EMOTIONS
AND STRESS

EMOTIONS
AND STRESS

HOW TO MANAGE THEM

DR KISHORE CHANDIRAMANI

PARTRIDGE

ISBN: Hardcover   978-1-4828-3646-2
               Softcover   978-1-4828-3645-5
               eBook   978-1-4828-3644-8

Print information available on the last page.

To order additional copies of this book, contact
Partridge India
000 800 10062 62
orders.india@partridgepublishing.com

www.partridgepublishing.com/india

CONTENTS

INTRODUCTION

This book brings together all the insights that I have come across in my life and found them helpful in dealing with my own stress and that of my clients. I see no major contradictions between modern psychiatric and psychological practices on one hand and the ancient traditions of mankind on the other. This book is an attempt to bring together all of those approaches under one umbrella and also to integrate them as far as possible.

I have found these approaches work for clients suffering from almost all forms of psychiatric problems, psychosomatic disorders, relationship issues, work-related stresses and also for individuals who do not suffer from any psychiatric problems, as some chapters address the existential issues that afflict all human beings, which may be in different proportions.

There are also spiritual elements that reduce stress, facilitate promotion of mental health and allow access to inner peace.

ABOUT THE AUTHOR

Dr Kishore Chandiramani has worked as a psychiatrist for more than thirty years across cultures and countries. He has tried to understand the mind from a number of different perspectives and this quest led him to study not just psychology and psychiatry but also philosophy and spiritual practices. He is currently in private practice in England and runs a stress management programme (Chandiramani, 2014) both for psychiatric patients as well as for psychologically healthy individuals who want to increase their immunity to stress.

DEDICATION

I dedicate this book to the late Mr S. N. Goenka, my Vipassana meditation teacher who taught me a new way of being in this world, which has helped me work on my emotional baggage and also taught me how not to create new stress in my mind. "I understand Mr Goenka went through the whole book and was pleased to give his approval and blessings".

This book brings together insights from modern science as well as ancient spiritual and philosophical traditions with the sole objective of helping people deal better with emotions and psychological stress.

Dr Kishore Chandiramani

CHAPTER 1

What Is Stress?

"People are not disturbed by things, but by the view they take of them"; this nearly 2000-year-old quote from Epictetus, a Greek philosopher, has received support from scientific research in recent years. Research suggests that individuals who do not perceive a stressful situation as stressful are very much less likely to experience the adverse effects and are able to cope better with stressful events. This does not mean that the actual quantum of the demand is immaterial; it does play a part if the demands cross a certain threshold for the individuals. It's just that the scientific opinion supports the notion that the perception is more important than the actual quantum of the demands.

We see ourselves taking different views of the same thing at different times, at times just the opposite of each other. We see someone as friendly and caring in the morning and a few hours later realise that they have been very selfish, unhelpful and uncaring. How to know which of these two thoughts represents the reality?

Just because a thought is there in my mind does not mean that it represents the reality out there or my true feelings. It may be a random thought, a wild thought, an adopted thought, an induced thought; and, as opposed to all of those, a thought that truly represents my core identity and inner feelings.

Unfortunately, we become advocates of our thoughts as soon as they enter our minds, leaving very little room to challenge them. Different forms of therapies and meditative practices, including Vipassana, help us recognise our true feelings and thoughts and they also help us see the reality as it is and not as it appears to be. This can enable us to deal with situations more appropriately, thereby reducing our stress.

Stress is defined as the gap between one's perception of the demands placed upon the individual and one's ability to cope with it. It's a very popular term and almost everyone understands it. Almost all psychological problems, be it anxiety, depression, anger or relationship problems, are forms of stress and the use of this term does not help distinguish one from another. When discussing mental illness, the word stress often causes more confusion, as it fails to convey the precise nature of the problem.

Mental health professionals use the term "stress disorders" only when they fail to categorise the condition into the neat categories of anxiety disorder, depressive illness, obsessive-compulsive disorder, etc.

To simplify the matter one can say that stress is an overarching term and it manifests differently in different individuals depending upon their personalities and mental state. It is the cause and also the end result of psychological disorders. The same stress can cause eczema in one person and alcoholism in another, depending upon their mental makeup.

Stress can therefore be understood in terms of the following three ways:

- As a stimulus: Environmental events such as war, earthquake, famine and accidents can cause stress even when the coping abilities of the individual are good.
- As a response (mental and physiological reaction): A stress-prone person experiences high levels of stress even in situations considered normal by most individuals.
- As an interaction between the individual and the environment (e.g. relationship problems).

A washing machine for the mind: Most of our daily actions and interactions produce stress, as our psyche is mobilised from the resting state to a state of action in order to meet a demand. The pure mind gets exposed to the environment and picks up stress, very much like our clothes, which pick up dust and grease during the course of the day. We put our clothes in a washing machine for cleaning and the cycle takes about an hour or two.

What about our minds? Where is the washing machine for the mind? What do we do to undo the stress? Just as we wash our clothes every day, we need to de-stress ourselves every day.

Stress management should be seen as a "prevention" rather than a "cure" of a problem when it has already resulted in illness. It should be practised daily, similar to cleaning our teeth every morning. We clean our teeth every day irrespective of whether they feel clean or unclean. In a similar fashion we need to practise stress management strategies even when we don't suffer from any stress disorder.

I normally ask people what they do to de-stress themselves and a common answer I get is, "I fix a drink or switch the television on." Unfortunately, there is very little scientific evidence that these two activities will undo stress. We feel that way because these are step-down activities rather than anti-stress ones. Drinking alcohol creates a wall between us and our inner selves so that we don't feel stressed; watching television distracts us from our normal preoccupations and worrying thoughts, but makes our minds react emotionally in a subtle way that we don't perceive as stress.

Most people who experience stress do not have a psychiatric illness and do not require professional help, but it is a condition that requires proper understanding and careful self-management as it could affect almost every aspect of one's life and eventually lead to psychiatric illness.

The following could be used as a rough guide to assess your stress levels.

Knowing how you feel first thing in the morning: You are connected to the inner most reaches of your mind during sleep and how you feel soon after waking is a good parameter of your inner mental life. Clients with high levels of stress report feeling unwell, unrefreshed or tired first thing in the morning and the feeling may disappear soon after, as we get busy with the activities of the day. Just because we do not feel stressed during the day does not mean we do not suffer from stress, as it is likely that we operate successfully in the external world from the superficial layers of our consciousness during our daily life, hence remain cut off from inner stress until a breakdown occurs.

How you feel at work: Occasionally wishing you did not have to come to work and wanting to go home can be normal, but if this happens often, it can signal stress. Feeling the need for frequent cups of coffee, tea or smoking to keep you going and being desperate for a holiday only a few months after the last one can be a sign of stress.

How you feel at the end of the day: Stress can manifest as tiredness, exhaustion and having headaches at the end of the day. If, after returning home and relaxing for a while, you still want to relax and do nothing, this could be a sign of stress. Not being able to have a life after five could be a sign of stress.

Frequent unpleasant dreams and nightmares: It is normal to experience both pleasant as well as unpleasant dreams, but if the proportion of unpleasant dreams is higher than that of pleasant ones some action is required even though the stress does not interfere with one's everyday life.

Anxiety and panic: Panic typically manifests as intense fear or discomfort that develops abruptly and reaches a peak within ten minutes. It is characterised by palpitations, sweating, trembling, sensation of shortness of breath, choking, chest pain, dizziness, light-headedness, fear of losing control and dying, etc. Panic attacks force clients to disengage from whatever they are doing in order to deal with the anxiety.

How you feel at the weekend: When you haven't planned a lot of activities can be a parameter of one's stress. A leisurely weekend can put us in touch with our inner being and not being able to connect with the inner joy can be a sign of stress as it is normally the stress that blocks our access to inner peace and tranquillity.

Stress can manifest differently in different individuals. For some it manifests as not being comfortable with their own company – they are always seeking company or some activity in order to avoid being on their own as they cannot tolerate solitude; whereas for others it can manifest as not wanting to be with people and they withdraw into their own shell. This can be explained on the basis of different personalities.

The extroverts find that their batteries are charged when they are with people or doing something, hence, when stressed, they seek the company of others.

For introverts, on the other hand, stress manifests as an accentuation of their tendency to withdraw into their own shell. Social contact can lead to more stress for them and, as a result, they avoid interacting with others.

Relationship and sexual difficulties: For some individuals, the first sign of stress is problems in their relationships. Denial of the stress that one feels within oneself can then result in its projection on to a relationship, resulting in being overcritical and intolerant of others, being irritable and angry and having sexual problems.

It is interesting to note that stress affects men and women differently; men report erectile problems and ejaculatory difficulties when stressed, whereas for women loss of desire is a common symptom of stress. We do not know why men do not suffer from desire problems as much as women do when under stress.

Overeating, increase in smoking and drinking: Eating brings a sense of comfort and relief from anxiety, which is used by some individuals to manage their stress. It does not neutralise the stress, but makes it disappear for a short while. Similarly, drinking alcohol creates a temporary wall between you and your stress and the feelings of stress return as soon as the effect wears off.

Psychological disorders: Difficulty making decisions, forgetfulness, accident proneness, inability to concentrate, anger, crying spells, feeling helpless and powerless, irritability, impulsive acts, frequent mood swings, loneliness, negative thinking and hopelessness are all symptoms of stress. Suffering from all these could indicate high levels of stress and it may or may not be severe enough to warrant a psychiatric diagnosis. It is only when these cause significant distress and incapacitation in everyday life and the individual cannot shake them off that a psychiatric diagnosis is made.

Suffering from a psychosomatic illness: Stress-prone individuals report higher rates of bodily symptoms, such as aches and pains, indigestion, allergies, headaches, backaches and they interpret these symptoms as indicative of a physical illness even though all the investigations are within the normal range. However, some individuals go on to develop medical disorders wherein stress plays an important part. Individuals suffering from illnesses such as migraines, hypertension, diabetes, asthma, irritable bowel syndrome, menopausal hot flushes, premenstrual tension, arthritis, etc. can have stress symptoms, which could be either the cause, consequence or just a reflection of the disease process. Stress management strategies can improve the prognosis of these disorders.

Experience of stress

Stress can be experienced at two levels: mental and physical. The relative degrees to which one experiences stress as a body symptom or mental event depend upon one's psychological mindedness and connection to their own body.

Stress can be experienced as a mental conflict leading to indecision, excessive worries, fear, poor concentration, mental anguish, irritability, anger, low moods, sense of helplessness and hopelessness, etc. Alternatively, stress can also be experienced at the physical level in the form of aches and pains, changes in physiological functions of the heart, intestines, lungs, muscles, skin, etc.

This knowledge helps us understand the following two broad approaches to managing stress:

- Psychological approaches, such as counselling and psychotherapy.
- Physiological approaches – Managing stress at the body (physiological) level by way of biofeedback, breath regulation, body-mind therapies, etc.

Clients who experience more bodily (autonomic) symptoms of stress and anxiety, such as palpitations, hyperventilation, cold and sweaty hands, stomach churning and chest pain, are more likely to respond to biofeedback therapies and body work, whereas those who experience stress in the form of psychic conflicts are more likely to respond to psychotherapy. However, there is some evidence to suggest that a combination of biofeedback with psychotherapy can result in a better outcome.

Models of Stress

Stress can be understood in terms of the following models:

Tiredness/mental fatigue

Stress can result from our minds not having enough time and skills to recuperate or heal following a period of activity. Just as after a very busy day we want to chill out and do nothing physically, we need similar breaks for our minds as well. The mind never rests; it is constantly thinking, planning and dreaming even during periods of rest. The only time when our mind rests fully is when it is awake and is in an emotionally neutral state – neither too happy nor too sad. Unfortunately, we are always seeking some or the other excitement to feel happy, thereby giving little time to the mind to heal itself.

Modern technology, including mobile devices, has made it even more difficult for us to completely switch off and distance ourselves from our worldly and tiring concerns.

Unfulfilled potential

Not being able to do what one is capable of or supposed to do can result in stress. This is the opposite of the tiredness model and relates to not doing something rather than doing things. Each individual is unique and it would be reasonable to assume that nature has given each one of us a unique potential to carry out certain tasks in our lifetime. Due to our unique individuality and the situation in this world, there are certain things that only we can do. Not doing the things that we are capable of can result in guilt and depression. However, it may be a difficult task to know one's true calling, the purpose why we are here.

Desire

Desires are the spice of life; we wouldn't want to live without them. This makes us invent new desires when the old ones are fulfilled. In fact, a desire-free state would be the most relaxed state to be in. We do not feel okay when nothing much is happening in our lives. As a result, our minds are never free from thinking, planning, seeking, creating new emotions and excitement, etc. These apparently positive endeavours also result in stress, which we can describe as a positive stress. The unfulfilled desires cause enormous stress, especially if we cannot forgo them or work towards alternative goals. Unfortunately, each desire attained also creates further stress by creating room for further desires that are yet to be fulfilled.

Relationship model

Relationships can cause stress in two totally opposite ways: as a result of not feeling connected or feeling isolated and as a result of being in an enmeshed relationship and feeling overwhelmed by them.

Existential model

Existentialism is a branch of philosophy that believes that stress is an integral part of life and cannot be avoided. It goes a step further in saying that the real stress of being a human being is much greater than what we normally appreciate.

Life apparently seems unfair. It is difficult to comprehend why people are struck with tragedies, sickness and financial ruin for no fault of their own. Very carefully planned lives are shattered by the cruel hand of destiny. A good life is guaranteed to no one and, in spite of our best efforts, we remain subject to chance and uncertainties. How can we feel secure in this world?

We probably live in denial for most of our lives and organise our lives in such a way that we do not confront this existential stress that is linked with our mortality, search for meaning in life, sense of responsibility, freedom of choice and ultimate fate.

According to existentialism a constant awareness of this type of stress is desirable as it makes us more human and our lives richer. Inability to acknowledge and accept this stress can result in clinical anxiety.

Strong negative emotions

This model is very close to the desire model as unfulfilled desires lead to negative emotions. It is not the intensity of the negative emotions that is linked to stress but our inability to process them. This is closely linked to our value system, world view, cultural beliefs, core identities and life goals. These factors dictate what would/would not be acceptable to us.

Control model

Wanting to be in control of our own and others' lives all the time can result in high levels of stress. We do not have full control over the results of our actions, as a lot of outside factors come into play in deciding the outcome. We can only control our actions. It is therefore important to make a distinction between our actions and their results, and change our focus from being result-orientated to action-orientated. Surrendering our preoccupation with getting the right results to our destiny can be helpful in this regard.

Physiological model

Our nervous system is composed of two different subsystems: the central nervous system and the autonomic nervous system. The autonomic nervous system is further divided into two groups: the sympathetic nervous system and the parasympathetic nervous system.

We experience stress at the body level in the form of sympathetic nervous system over-activity or an imbalance between the sympathetic and parasympathetic nervous system activation.

Normally both these systems work in harmony, very much like the accelerator and the brake in our car. But in stress situations there is an imbalance between the two. It is possible to correct this imbalance by means of biofeedback treatment and certain body-mind therapies.

Spiritual/religious model

In a nutshell, this world that we perceive through our five senses is not enough to make us happy. Unfortunately, most of us realise this only after spending a lifetime chasing achievements of the external world.

In everyday life we tend to identify ourselves with the apparent systems that are finite (i.e. our body, family, possessions, environment and people), but at a deeper level our existence is linked with and supported by the infinite cosmic forces that support our life on this planet. Finding a meaningful connection with the infinite is considered very important for our well-being in most spiritual traditions. Getting too immersed into the concerns of this world and losing this connection with the infinite can make us vulnerable to stress that can result from the vicissitudes of life.

Genetic/biological model

For some individuals genetic and biological factors play a major role compared to the environmental ones in producing stress. These factors modulate release of certain chemicals such as serotonin and adrenaline, which are involved in producing anxiety and depression.

Autonomic Nervous System and Stress

Our nervous system consists of two separate parts: one that is under our control is called the central nervous system, which controls functions such as hand movements, and the other, which is not under our control, is called the autonomic nervous system, which is responsible for regulating the functions such as gut movements, heart beats, blood flow in our arteries, respiratory rhythms, skin temperatures, brain waves, etc. Until recently it was believed that apart from very few functions, such as respiration, muscle tension, etc., we cannot control these functions, but with the advent of biofeedback treatments it has become possible for us to control these functions as well. This research has had important implications in stress management as the stress that we experience inside our bodies results from alterations in the autonomic functions.

The autonomic nervous system can be broadly divided into the following two subsystems:

1. Sympathetic nervous system: This is involved in dealing with emergencies, such as fear, fight and flight. It puts our system in hyper drive by accelerating the heart rate, blood flow into muscles and our respiratory rate. This system enables us to deal with any emergency.
2. Parasympathetic nervous system: This plays the important functions of healing, regeneration and nurturance in times of rest. It slows down the heart and respiration rates and increases movements of intestines. It also results in increased blood flow to skin thereby increasing skin temperature.

It is important for normal functioning of our psyche that these two systems function in harmony with each other. Any imbalance in the two systems can result in illness. An increase in sympathetic activity can result in anxiety/panic attacks, hypertension, irritable bowel disease, premature ejaculation, etc. and a hyperactivity of parasympathetic activity can result in illnesses such as bronchial asthma, syncope and chronic fatigue syndrome.

CHAPTER 2

What Causes Stress?

Poverty is stressful; being rich and famous is also stressful
Not having friends is stressful; having too many friends is also stressful
Living alone is stressful; being a householder is also stressful
Being unemployed is stressful; having a job is also stressful
Not having any children is stressful; having children is also stressful
Doing the right thing is stressful; not doing it is also stressful.

Nearly every situation is associated with some stress. Life without stress is inconceivable as stress cannot be avoided no matter what we do or choose not to do.

The opposite of it is also true, that almost every situation offers a set of opportunities, doing something offers opportunities and not doing it offers a different set of opportunities; being a householder offers opportunities and living a solitary life also offers opportunities. Keeping our focus on the opportunities can be a way of coping with stress.

Just as it is normal to feel stressed, it is only normal that one makes constant efforts to manage it more effectively. If left unmanaged, stress can lead to emotional, psychological and even physical illnesses, sometimes not known even to the person themselves, and also to health professionals and scientists. Psychological stress affects us in more ways than we normally acknowledge.

Have I bitten off more than I can chew?

I hardly say anything more than a "hello" or "how are you" to my neighbours.

*I don't even know the personal and family details of
people I have worked closely with for years.*

I have got about twenty friends, but no time for intimate talk.

I multitask – watch television and read the newspaper whilst I am eating.

I receive texts/emails/phone calls at least once every ten minutes; is it too many?

I use my mobile phone even in my bedroom and bathroom; is it inappropriate?

I work six days a week and sometimes late nights preparing reports.

I go on holiday only once a year for a couple of weeks; is it too little time?

*I have no time for the books and movies of my interest
that have been released in recent months.*

*I hardly think about issues such as the purpose of life, the meaning in
relationships, my true calling and what will become of me after death.*

Is it all too much and too stressful for me?

Overwork can cause stress, but the perception of it plays a greater role. Stress is our response to a demanding situation that we feel unable to cope with.

People who have studied the human mind in greater depth tell us that a simple awareness of a situation does not cause stress. If that were so, then everyone who becomes aware of a difficult situation should be stressed. The fact that they don't indicates that our perception and judgements play a major role in the experience of stress.

Types of Stress

Stress in response to a life situation

It is possible to understand the majority of our stressful experiences as resulting from our encounters with difficult life situations and there is an element of understandability there. We create new negative experiences when we are faced with those situations. It is possible to put a stop to the stress by dealing with situations, objects and people without making strong judgements about them or by distracting ourselves into something else, even though it may be a negative situation for us. We have a bit more control over these experiences.

Stress that appears out of the blue

Clients who suffer from panic disorder say that they can't understand their anxiety in terms of what is going on in their lives. It is the emotion that comes first, out of the blue, and makes them interpret things, including their normal bodily functions and sensations, as abnormal and harmful. This stress is different from the one discussed earlier. It may be that this stress is related to our childhood experiences, faulty learning or identifications with an adult figure who suffered with stress. We can understand this type of stress in terms of a replaying of past emotions that were created in response to a difficult situation. It may be that these emotions were not worked through properly by our mind at the time and they went into the unconscious mind with all their emotional charge. I call them ghost emotions.

Stress that has an element of absurdity

Clients with phobias and obsessive-compulsive disorder experience a stress that appears, even to them, as absurd and irrational. It can be understood in terms of evolutionary anxiety that our forefathers had in relation to the natural human fears and insecurities; these were relevant in their times and protective of life, and are passed on to us through our genes or collective unconscious mind. The stress of phobias and OCD can also be explained on the basis of displacement of a real life concern from their original context on to something innocuous. The obsessive-compulsive disorder generally has a strong genetic component to it.

Biological stress

One can also experience stress as a result of physical insult to the brain or certain chemical changes in the body. For example, clients with brain tumours or traumatic brain injury suffer from anxiety attacks and clients with hormonal changes during postpartum period or with thyroid problems suffer from depression. These can't be fully explained on the basis of life events.

So far, we have discussed stress mainly in terms of a mental reaction to something and this mental reaction is a consequence of how we perceive and judge different things in this world. One can ask why, in the first place, one person reacts in a certain way and not in other ways. Apart from genetic predisposition, we can understand this in terms of early childhood experiences. According to psychoanalysis, the software of our mind is written in the first five years of our lives and we keep re-playing that software for the rest of our lives. We can change that software by will later on in life.

Depression and Its Causes

It is difficult to distinguish clinical depression from normal sadness apart from its consequences and impact on the life of the individual, which may well be a reflection on the individual's ability to cope, rather than on the nature of the problem.

In simple terms, depression becomes clinical when it causes significant distress and interferes with our everyday life and it can't be shaken off. It assumes certain characteristics of a clinical state characterised by weight loss, loss of appetite, and loss of pleasure and motivation to do things.

A basic human condition

Gautama the Buddha understood human suffering as the basic human condition. This has been misunderstood by many as a nihilistic approach. Existentialism and psychoanalysis also believe that there are negative forces in our personalities that cannot be completely eliminated, very much like a sea bed that can't be wiped clean. Similarly the slate of our mind cannot be wiped clean. We should therefore negotiate our way in such a way that we are minimally affected by these negative forces. We come across a view contrary to this in most religions, including Buddhism. Almost all religions, including Christianity, Buddhism and Hinduism, remind us that it is possible to eliminate all suffering and achieve enlightenment or nirvana in this very lifetime by way of transcending our human ways of being.

Soren Kierkegaard (1849), a Danish philosopher, reminded us that all normal human beings are, at the very bottom of their existence, anxious, depressed and insecure. He said that in our normal consciousness we are unable to notice these deeper feelings. In this regard, depression can be seen as a natural emotion if it happens as a result of this awareness of the deeper self. It is only natural to feel small and helpless in this ever growing world in which we seem to have very little control over things. The sheer number of people inhabiting this planet and their suffering fill us with a sense of helplessness. It may be that the feelings of helplessness described by patients are just a disguised manifestation of this existential anguish and powerlessness, which the individual finds difficult to accept.

Paul Tillich (1952), an existential thinker, explains it further by saying that the depressed person is more sensitive to these problems of human existence and so feels profound emotions. Being unable to confront these emotions, they settle into a limited self-affirmation and restricted lifestyle. Their avoidance of this pain also leads to a restriction of the joys that one can experience.

Depression has also been viewed as a consequence of the individual's inability to come to terms with the unavoidable human pain. One can say that one third of all human suffering is unavoidable (ontological) and the remaining two-thirds (ontic) are there because one cannot accept the unavoidable one third and is trying hard to get it out of one's life.

Absence of meaning

Depression can be seen as a result of our inability to discover or create meaning in our lives or our failure to come to terms with the feelings of meaninglessness that we normally encounter at times. There are no blueprints for human life, no grand designs or maps that we can follow. We are free to become what we want to and create meanings through our actions and choices.

Psychiatrists generally see a sense of meaninglessness as a manifestation of depression whereas in existentialism (a branch of philosophy) it is understood as the cause of it. In an existential sense, meaning is seen as a by-product of one's engagement with this world and a failure to engage with the world could result in depression. This is, of course, a simplistic explanation of meaning.

Heidegger (1927), a German philosopher, saw the crisis of meaning as unavoidable to some extent. He understood human beings as constantly being caught between the two positions of "no longer" and "not yet", which can lead to a loss of meaning as whatever we have achieved becomes "no longer", taking away all the meanings with it. We know that different things matter to us at different times, but the fact that they do not hang together as some unified whole takes away their meaning.

An alienation from oneself

Heidegger (1927) has pointed out that the alienating influence of technology may be related to the phenomenon of rising depression in modern society. The remedy lies in a "return to our true nature" and staying connected with our inner world.

Increasing globalisation of culture

This has posed unique problems for the mental health professional. It does not seem to be producing cultural uniformity; rather it has resulted in feelings of confusion, isolation, loneliness and identity problems, which may be the additional factors contributing to the rise of depression. More and more people are being uprooted from their homelands as a result of migration and are leading lives of relative social isolation with a limited support system. From an existential perspective, it can be seen as an advantage as it offers opportunities to confront the basic human concerns. Without this work one remains vulnerable to depression. Todres (2002), in his article, has pointed out that religion, family and community life seem inadequate in addressing this task in recent times.

A medicalised social malady

It has been argued and with good reasons that to some extent we have medicalised unhappiness. Depression in this context can be seen as a social problem as it is closely linked with poor social support, family burden, poverty, divorce, drug abuse, urbanisation and modernisation, etc.

Society, culture and depression

Information technology has vastly increased the awareness of an average citizen about things happening elsewhere and as a result has increased the gap between "what is" and "what should be" in the outside world, and the internal tensions between "who I am" and "who I think I ought to be". Cultural factors play an important role in the causation of depression.

When a group of American psychologists met with the Dalai Lama, he asked what difficulties are most common for Americans. One of the most mentioned and strongest was self-hatred and low self-esteem. The Dalai Lama's reaction was incredulous as, according to him, self-hatred and low self-esteem are relatively unknown in Tibetan Culture (Kornfield, 2000).

Women and depression

Women are twice as likely to suffer from depression as men. Feminists have argued that to a large extent depression is not rooted in the biology and that the altered biology (reported in the literature) may be a concomitant of social, political and cultural forces operating in a given society. Women tend to seek help more often than men.

Losses of all kinds

Losing a parent in childhood has been associated with high rates of depression later in life. At times it is just a fear of loss or a symbolic stress that reminds us of past experiences of losses that brings on depression.

Having no attachment figures

Lack of attachment figures in childhood and frequent separations in adulthood, a history of having a disturbed relationship with one's own mother/ attachment figures in childhood are known to cause depression later on in life.

Problems in parenting

Instances such as high parental expectations and internalisation of those high expectations can cause depression. Secondly, being brought up in controlling environments and suffering from parental neglect can cause depression.

Adopting very high internal standards

Having expectations such as to be good and loving, superior and strong, and to be loved and worthy all the time can cause depression.

Inability to give up unattainable goals

This can cause depression. In relationships, it could be related to one's failure to elicit specific responses from specific people. The situation gets complicated when the alternatives to the expected response or behaviour are not acceptable to the individual.

No rewards

Depression can occur when a positive action does not bring about positive results. It is seen when the social environment does not provide sufficient rewards. One can argue against this position by saying that depression can result when one hasn't learnt the behaviour that could be suitably rewarded by others. Some investigators consider depression as a result of one's own inability to reward oneself.

Distance regulation

In relationships, depression can occur as a result of problems in distance regulation. The distance between two individuals should be optimal, like the strings of a guitar. Being too close or too far apart will not produce good music.

Biorhythms

Depression can cause disruption in one's daily rhythms – not eating enough and in time, irregular sleep–wake cycle, reduced physical activity, etc. All this can make depression worse.

Social isolation

Depressed individuals tend to withdraw from the outside world and other human beings, which results in a worsening of their depression. Increasing human contact and being more engaged with the outside world can be therapeutic.

Anxiety and Its Causes

Anxiety is generally a normal and adaptive response to a threat that prepares us for fight or flight. It becomes abnormal only when it is excessive or its timing is inappropriate with regard to the threat.

Anxiety and panic disorders are generally an over-learnt response to difficult situations. Anxiety invariably starts as a normal, justified response to a difficult situation and it serves the purpose of preparing the individual to meet an emergency situation (i.e. fear, fight or flight). However, over a period of time the emotional response gets set into our psyche and at times gets detached from its original context. This response then gets conditioned to mundane day-to-day activities or objects, leading to avoidance of the situation.

Life-threatening experiences: Going through an experience that is perceived as life-threatening for oneself or one's loved ones can cause anxiety. This could be being involved in an accident, child birth, undergoing major surgery, being diagnosed with a major illness, etc. Anxiety in these situations is justified and understandable. However, for some this anxiety response is over-learnt and it persists well beyond the natural time span. This can also be described as death anxiety. In the normal course of life we get acclimatised to the idea that one day we will all die and our loved ones will also die. Separation from our loved ones and loss are inevitable. Some individuals cannot come to terms with this human reality and as a result suffer from anxiety.

Parenting issues: Being brought up in a strict and disciplined environment. Children who perceive their parents as harsh and punitive are more likely to suffer from anxiety.

Having over-protective parents – the message given to the child is that this world is potentially a dangerous place and one has to be on guard all the time.

Caregivers who expect too much from children in their care can also induce anxiety in them. These standards are then internalised by the child and they come to expect too much from themselves even later on in life.

Threats of loss: Threat of loss or separation from loved ones. Individuals who have experienced separation from their parents or siblings several times in their childhood are more likely to suffer from anxiety.

Fear of losing control over oneself: Individuals who have had very poor control over their inner impulses of either aggressive or sexual nature remain in fear of these impulses. It may be that one's control of the unconscious impulses is normal, but the impulses are too many and too strong to handle. Anxiety can also result from not being able to satisfy one's basic needs and desires.

It will come back to haunt you if

You put your needs above those of your loved ones
You have been too busy to spend time with your family and real friends
You take advantage of others' ignorance and weakness
You betray people who have reposed their trust in you
You ignore the needs of people who are dependent on you
You let people take advantage of you
Your actions are making people unhappy
You tolerate injustice and can't face up to it
You choose not to actualise your full potential.

CHAPTER 3

Understanding the Mind

Is my obsession with work an escape from the dreadful loneliness of my existence or am I truly actualising my full potential?

Is my desire to succeed and be powerful compensating for my feelings of being small and helpless or am I genuinely ambitious?

Is my indifference to you an attempt to hide my attraction for you or am I truly uninterested?

Is my attempt to please you just a way of overcoming my fear of you or am I a genuinely pleasant person?

Is my politeness covering up my indifference to this world?

Is my rigid moral value system protecting me from an adventurous streak in me or am I truly a person of high moral values?

Is my anger with you a reflection of my deep attachment and identification with you, and the helplessness that comes with it, or is it a sign of my separateness and lack of empathy?

Is my being judgemental with you a genuine desire for your success and growth?

Is it not normal to feel depressed in this apparently indifferent and unfriendly world?

Is my charity compensating for my guilt?

How can I say that I have understood my mind fully without understanding my dreams? Aren't my dreams more bizarre than the symptoms my clients come up with, even the ones with psychosis? We can't understand the mind without taking into account the existence of the unconscious mind. It will not be possible to explain dreams, symptoms of psychosis, panic disorder, phobias, etc. without acknowledging the existence of the unconscious mind.

In order to understand the psychological symptoms and deal with them it is very important that we understand how the normal mind works.

Functioning of the Mind

The mind can be understood in terms of two broad compartments: the conscious and the unconscious. The conscious mind is just the tip of an iceberg and the rest is the unconscious. According to a rough estimate only about 10% to 20% of our mind is conscious and the rest is unconscious. The psychological implication of this is that when we experience extreme emotions we have to say to ourselves that we are talking about only 10% to 20% of the mind and the rest is unknown to us. The remaining 80% to 90% contains joys and sorrows that may be several times greater than the joys and sorrows we have ever experienced in our lifetime. Jung (1959), a Swiss psychologist, has described confronting this unconscious as the central task of human life.

In modern times the unconscious mind has been popularised by Sigmund Freud (1915). According to his psychoanalytic theories, we can't access the unconscious mind at will; it becomes accessible to us only in dreams, during psychotic episodes or under the influence of drugs, etc.

However, in some schools of thought, there is no belief in the unconscious and it is understood only in the terms of the unattended aspects of the mind, which can be accessed at any time. We can understand this using the example of a library. When we enter a library there are thousands of books lying folded on the shelves. These are like the unconscious mind and the book that is open in front of us is the conscious mind.

Another way to understand the unconscious mind is by visualising a dark room that we enter with a torch. The torch lights up only a small patch and the rest is dark and one can move the torch in different directions. Using this analogy for our mind, whatever is in the focus of the light is the conscious mind and the rest unconscious.

What is conscious today can become unconscious tomorrow and vice versa, and according to the psychoanalytic theory it is not under our control to move from conscious to unconscious. Sigmund Freud (1915) gave the example of a fountain: the water visible is the conscious mind and what is in the pond is the unconscious, and the two are in constant circulation.

Under normal circumstances the conscious mind, although small, has good control over the unconscious and there is a thick barrier between the two. This does not allow the unconscious to spill out in to the conscious mind. However, in certain situations (i.e. psychological stress or because of genetic factors) this barrier is weakened and the unconscious mind can spill out in to the conscious mind and that's when psychosis and some other psychiatric disorders occur.

We can also understand this model of the mind in terms of a horse and a horseman. The horse can be described as the unconscious mind and the horseman as the conscious mind. Under normal circumstances, the horseman has full control over the horse, but at certain times we find that the horse takes over and that's when psychotic illness occurs. A lot of the psychiatric symptoms can be explained in terms of the unconscious experiences entering into the conscious mind in an uncoordinated fashion.

It would be appropriate to discuss the unconscious mind in a little more detail here as it can help us make some sense of psychiatric symptoms. The unconscious mind is the storehouse of all our past experiences, thoughts, emotions, images, feelings, memories, etc., both stressful and neutral.

We collect thousands of experiences on a daily basis and many of them are stressful in nature. If we are good at managing this stress on a daily basis, a lot of them get worked on and do not leave any emotional residue, even though they are being recorded in the unconscious mind. However, if a stressful or emotionally charged experience does not get worked on it goes into the unconscious mind with all its emotional charge and stress in seed form.

Another example to explain this would be to say that the "camera of our mind" captures every moment of our life, not just in the form of pictures and sound, but all the five sense faculties plus our emotions and thoughts. The recordings (DVDs) of all these experiences are stored in our unconscious mind. This storage is different from the storage in a library where the DVDs are static and don't go through further changes. The DVDs stored in the unconscious mind constantly go through changes, and emotions can jump from one DVD to another. That explains how emotions from a really stressful but shameful experience are displaced on to innocuous experiences so that they get worked on, otherwise the painful experiences will never get worked on due to the reluctance of the conscious mind to revisit them. It may also be the case that emotions from an experience related to a problem that is perceived by the individual as unsolvable are shifted on to a problem that can be solved (e.g. relationship problems manifesting as compulsive cleaning of the house).

These DVDs from the unconscious mind keep getting replayed in different situations that act as triggers for them to come out into the conscious mind. Each time a past experience is replayed it is modified by the new experiences that we are forming all the time as the new experience merges with the old one and an edited version of the old DVD is formed. This edited version is then stored in the unconscious mind. Next time when this DVD is replayed it might undergo further modifications depending upon the nature of the new experience. Unfortunately, for some individuals these old painful emotions are constantly replayed without getting modified as the person has not made any conscious effort to change them.

Evidently we collect millions of such experiences in a lifetime and they are all stored in the unconscious mind. What happens to these experiences in the unconscious mind depends upon what sort of environment they get in there. It's like whether someone is going into a university or a prison. If these new experiences get a corrective environment like that of a university they go through a process of neutralisation and healing. The process of dreaming does this kind of neutralisation work on these experiences.

However, on the contrary, if these new experiences, upon entering the unconscious mind, come into contact with a lot of stressful experiences already there, they join hands with them and proliferate. They begin to sprout as if the seed has found a fertile soil. It is very much like someone going into prison as a petty criminal and coming out a hardened criminal. The seeds of these experiences start proliferating and these experiences come back into the conscious mind in the form of psychiatric symptoms (i.e. panic attacks, obsessions, compulsions, paranoid thoughts, etc.). Patients feel that these experiences come out of the blue, but truly speaking these are the exaggerated versions of their own thoughts and feelings that they had in the past.

Multiple layers of consciousness

You might be familiar with some days when we get up with headaches or body aches and as we get ready to go to work these recede back and we are able to function well at work. The symptom comes back when we return home and want to relax.

Some individuals report experiencing stress only after the stressful event was over. The real tiredness of a court case or a marriage ceremony is felt only after the event. It's because the mind is made up of multiple layers of consciousness and we shift from one level to another, depending upon the time of the day and the demands of the situation we are in.

We are normally conscious of only the superficial layers of consciousness and may not feel the pain or stress that is hidden in the deeper reaches of the mind. Experiencing the deeper discomfort is better than staying detached from it as working through it can lead to a heightened sense of well-being.

The conscious v unconscious: the balancing act

According to psychoanalytic theories, the unconscious mind always tries to compensate for the excesses of the conscious mind, and vice versa. Too much unconscious hostility can make a person very polite on the surface and too much suppression of desires can lead to a compensatory revolt from the unconscious mind in the form of a psychotic breakdown. The denials of conscious mind can manifest in the form of hallucinatory experiences, reminding the individual of their psychological reality, although in an exaggerated and maladaptive way. A conscious awareness of one's unconscious helplessness and powerlessness can create a strong achievement motivation in the conscious mind that compensates for the deficiencies. Every psychiatric symptom has a purpose and invariably they are about protection of the individual, although not entirely appropriate to the times and the circumstances as they are governed by past conditionings.

The nature of psychosis

Psychosis can be understood only when we take in to account the existence of the unconscious mind. Without a belief in the unconscious we cannot understand psychosis. It is the unconscious that brings forth our dreams and it is outside the realms of time, space and rationality. It is the storehouse of all of our past experiences – our joys, fears, worries, sadness, secrets, etc. It also contains exaggerated and distorted images of our fears and fantasies that provide the material for development of psychotic symptoms. Psychotic symptoms can also be seen as the expression of the censored parts of our unconscious mind. It is full of all the unpleasant aspects that we do not even want to admit to ourselves. It is also the storehouse of all the sublime and joyful experiences that one can experience in this lifetime. It is the unconscious that connects us to a larger universal mind from which it can draw both positive and negative thoughts.

The unconscious mind has a much larger capacity than the conscious mind, but it is the conscious mind that keeps the unconscious in check. It is very much like the horse and the horseman where the horse represents the unconscious mind and the horseman the conscious mind. Normally the horseman is in full control of the horse, but in a psychotic state it is the horse that takes over the horseman and takes him to places he may not want to go.

The unconscious mind can be understood in terms of two separate sections; the personal unconscious and the collective unconscious. The personal unconscious is nothing but a collection of our own past experiences, and the collective unconscious is like an ocean or the universal mind that stores information beyond what the individual has experienced in their lifetime. In view of this, the symptoms of psychosis can be understood in terms of two broad categories:

1. Exaggeration of our own fears, denials, projections and suspicions. These are stored in the personal unconscious.
2. Symptoms that are totally bizarre and alien to us. These can be understood in terms of the workings of the collective unconscious, where symptoms filter through from transpersonal realms.

CHAPTER 4

Our Emotions: Friends or Foes

"All emotions reveal our mind to ourselves but hide the true life from us."
The Bhagvad Gita (1994)

"What a foe may do to a foe,
Or a hater to a hater –
Far worse than that
The mind ill held may do to him.

Not mother, father, nor even other kinsmen
May do that good to him
Far better than that
The mind well held may do to him."

The Dhammapada (1987)

Emotions are the spice of life; they give meaning to everything that we experience and they are the substrate of almost all our experiences.

We cannot imagine a life without emotions; it would not be worth living. They bring joys and ecstasies to us; they bring divine and sublime experiences to us; they bring meaning to life and make it worth living. However, what a pity – it is these very emotions that drive people to commit suicide, kill their fellow beings, torture and rape them. Human suffering is largely dependent upon how we feel in different situations.

Dealing with our emotions should be one of our top priorities. Unfortunately, our parents and teachers only tell us what is the right way of thinking, feeling and doing things, but they seldom teach us how not to worry, not to be angry, anxious or depressed. "Don't worry, be happy" is easier said than done.

The rainbow of emotions

Have you ever felt happy or sad for no apparent reason? How do you explain it? Is it because you got out of bed on the wrong side in the morning? Was it driven by some chemical changes happening as a result of some illness? Or was it just a feeling that your unconscious mind created and you had no access to the location and cause of its origin?

All the different types of emotions can be divided into four broad categories:

- pleasant
- unpleasant
- mixed
- neither pleasant nor unpleasant

The unpleasant emotions are not necessarily unhelpful as there are times when they help us more than the pleasant ones, and the pleasant ones can be harmful to us on certain occasions.

Understanding Emotions

> *There is no shame in feeling depressed, anxious or angry, but it would be a shame if we got stuck in them.*

The emotions that we experience at a given point in time could be:

A replay of a past emotion that was recorded in our mind:

Everything that we experience gets recorded in our mind, very much like recordings on a tape recorder, and these emotions get stored in our unconscious mind. These mood states can get activated from time to time and they seem to appear out of the blue. We cannot understand these mood states on the basis of what is going on in our lives.

It is best not to participate in them and let the emotion run its course without reacting mentally to it. We can stop our mental reactions to these re-lived experiences by understanding the emotions in terms of their impermanent nature and not identifying with them. Non-identification can be achieved by saying to oneself, "This is not the real me; I am not this emotion. This emotion is crossing my mind and doesn't belong to my real self." It may be a result of a random or unrealistic thought. Bringing the opposite mood state to undo the thought can be counter-productive as the original emotion might slip back into the unconscious mind unaltered and it can reappear at any time later on.

A new emotion that was created at the time of experiencing it:

We constantly create new emotions in response to the situation we are in and also as a result of our desires, fears and the judgements that we make about ourselves and others. We can understand these emotions on the basis of what is going on in our lives and in our conscious mind.

Distracting our minds and/or creating an opposite emotion by thinking or doing something can be helpful if we want to stop the negative emotion getting stronger. Being non-judgemental about things and keeping a bigger picture in mind can stop the process of creation of new strongly negative emotions.

Impact of the environment (stress in the air):

Stress that is in the air can be perceived by us. Certain places and people have specific auras that impinge on our well-being. I have had friends who tell me that just travelling on the London Underground makes them stressed. Another example could be the stress around Christmas time in the Western world and any festival time elsewhere, which can be felt even by those who do not celebrate it. We know from our own experience that spending time with certain people can have a depleting effect on our psyche, whereas a few minutes spent with a positive person can make us feel good about ourselves and good about this world. The same principle works when people want to visit temples, churches, sacred places or go on a pilgrimage as the experience there can undo stress.

You must be aware that we all have mental pictures of certain places we visited in the past and these get frozen in our minds although we do not understand anything significant happening there at that point in time.

Making a list of situations that enrich you and the ones that deplete you can be helpful. Spending a few minutes every day imagining being with people and in places where you felt calm can be helpful.

Dealing with Emotions

We can manage our moods better if we are not completely submerged in the emotion that we are experiencing at any given point in time, which happens quite often. Emotions are absolutistic in nature. They split things in black and white and don't let us see the grey shades. The truth is that the reality lies somewhere in between. Wisdom dawns on us only when the mood and the situation have gone by and we did not act appropriately in time.

It would therefore be desirable that we can free a part of our mind from what is going on inside it, in order to have a foothold on reality. The easiest way to do that is to start observing the emotion without judging it or participating in it.

You can change your emotions by changing your thoughts. It seems that more than 80% of the thoughts that come automatically to our minds do not represent the reality out there in totality and need some fine tuning. The solution to this problem is, whenever you get any thought, no matter how wise or rational it appears to you, say to yourself that "it may be unrealistic, I am not discarding it but putting it on the back burner of my mind for now".

During the next few minutes try to say to yourself that the opposite of this thought can also be true to some extent. If there is truth in your original thought it will come back to you, and this time may be in a refined form (i.e. more realistic than the original thought).

Synthesis of the opposites

> *My family is my salvation and it is my bondage.*
> *My spouse is my headache and she is my balm.*
> *My children are my hopes and they are my worries.*
> *My body is a prison and it is also a temple.*
> *My mind is a trap and it's also a tool for my liberation.*
> *My parents helped me grow and they also set a limit to my growth.*
> *Money gave me happiness and it also gave me grief.*
> *Music and sex elevate me and they also pull me down.*
> *My work keeps me sane and it also drives me crazy.*

Taking personal things in an impersonal manner

Imagine that what you are going through is happening not to you but to someone else (i.e. a friend, a neighbour or a relative) and they are sitting next to you. What advice would you give to them? See if you could give the same advice to yourself.

Understand every emotion in terms of its transitory nature, treating your emotions as the weather that keeps changing and having no control over them. Just as you go about your business in spite of the adverse weather knowing that it will change sooner or later.

Dealing with Specific Emotions

Pleasure and excitement

How sad that all the pleasures of life will continue to be there when I am gone; how can I fit all possible pleasures into this one lifetime?

How do we cope when good experiences come to an end? Generally we create new desires and chase new happiness and it keeps us going. Sometimes we feel happy for no obvious reason. When pleasant past experiences are reactivated in our minds we feel happy for no apparent reason. This happiness comes out of the blue. It is good to have many such experiences every day, but the downside of having these experiences is that they colour our judgement and make us unrealistically optimistic, thereby interfering with our ability to cope with the reality.

There is no need to stop these experiences, and no one would want to do that, but if we could rescue a part of our mind that has to make decisions and act from this emotionally neutral consciousness, it will keep us firmly grounded in the reality.

The next big question is how to rescue a part of our mind from pleasurable experience – it is best done by observing these emotions in a non-judgemental and detached manner as discussed in other sections of this book.

Guilt

Guilt is generally about something that we did or did not do in the past and feeling personally responsible for any wrong-doings. There are two types of guilt: clinical guilt that arises from wrong-doings and personal failures and existential guilt that is about not doing the right thing and not using our full potential; the things that we are capable of doing and haven't done so far. It's about our unrealised potential rather than about having done something wrong. Both these types of guilt can be remedied.

The best way to deal with clinical guilt is to understand the past in terms of historical inevitability – things had to happen that way, they could not have happened any other way. It doesn't mean that we deny our responsibilities – our responsibility lies in learning our lessons from the experience and doing things differently in the future.

There is a saying in Zen Buddhism that "we cannot not make mistakes, but we must learn how to make mistakes perfectly". It's about not losing our emotional balance, no matter what situation we are in, and learning our lessons.

Judging ourselves in terms of our intentions and not actions: Often we end up feeling guilty because in spite of our best intentions we could not do the right thing or our actions did not have the desired result. At times, our well-meaning actions are perceived as unhelpful by people who want to induce guilt in us. It is important to note here that we can only control our actions and not the results of them. Whether a person can benefit from our actions or not depends on their destinies as well. We set out to help people close to us, but not everyone gets the benefit in the same way – that's life.

In certain situations, no amount of *thinking* can take away the guilt as some *action* is required to undo the guilt. Writing down a plan to carry out a specific remedial action can be helpful.

Some individuals are very sensitive and you cannot not hurt them. No matter what you do they will be hurt. Even your best intentions to help them will be perceived by them as antagonistic and hostile. Accept it as a fact of life without feeling guilty. It should not make us give up our good intentions.

The old proverb "the road to hell is paved with good intentions" is said, in my opinion, to encourage people to follow through their intentions with appropriate actions. It should not be seen as inducement not to have good intentions.

Low self-esteem and lack of confidence

Self-esteem is commonly understood in terms of an entity and quantity. Confidence is seen as a way of behaving that has to be learned from others like a new language. A number of strategies have been developed to boost one's self-esteem. The emphasis seems to be on doing something or achieving something on which one can hang one's self-esteem. Contrary to this position, the spiritual and existential approaches believe that all that really matters is already given to us. In fact, what is generally described as self-confidence is a put-on behaviour, which may be a result of a denial of the realities of human life. It may even be counterproductive as it takes a person away from the natural state of affairs, which brings humility.

We are all born with reasonably good self-esteem, which gets damaged during the course of our life. The support for this argument comes from watching animals – seeing a horse gallop, a lion roar or a bird fly – they haven't attended any self-esteem lessons or confidence-boosting classes. This understanding is reassuring as it removes the burden of learning new strategies or roles in order to behave confidently.

We create low self-esteem by thinking and doing things in certain ways that affect our innate confidence. We are guided by a mental picture of how things should be and try to compare it with the reality. All that we need to do is to give up our habitual way of interpreting things and allow our true nature to come out.

Comparisons with others can lower one's self-esteem. If that is the case, try to analyse whether the achievements of the other person relate to your life and its goals or not. If yes, then this low self-esteem can be converted into inspiration, which will bring positive feelings. Otherwise it can be treated as an unrelated meaningless comparison that is easy to discard.

Anger/resentment

> *Seeing people as imperfect – we are not perfect, how can we expect others to be perfect?*

Justified anger hurts as much as unjustified anger, hence it is best to deal with all types of anger irrespective of whether it is justified or unjustified.

Whatever we achieve by getting angry can also be achieved without getting angry.

Wrong-doers cannot escape the consequences of their action. We can unburden ourselves by leaving the matter to nature or to God (for those who have faith in God).

Mentally rehearse angry statements we have made in the past by rephrasing the statements and saying them without being angry. Think about a person who rarely gets angry and imagine how they would have responded to this situation.

There is an element of optimism about anger as underneath it there is a desire to set things right. A small dose of realistic pessimism about things can help us deal with anger more appropriately. If we can't do it on our own, we can ask a friend to paint a gloomy, but realistic picture of the scenario we are in.

If the anger is directed towards a particular person, think of the worst possible scenario, make a list of even worse things that the person was capable of doing and chose not to do. I saw a client recently who had a lot of angry thoughts towards his spouse. These related to everyday irritations and differences of opinion. I could see that deep down they both loved each other. I encouraged them to make a list of all the unpleasant and harmful things their spouse was not doing, the things other couples do to each other, looking through their history and their own acquaintances.

Seeing the hand of our own destiny in others' actions

In certain cultures people are encouraged to believe that no human being is given the authority to write somebody else's destiny; we are given the powers only to change our own destiny by carrying out the right action. If someone has been successful in causing harm to us it must be destined, otherwise that person would not have been successful. They simply became the medium and will have to face the consequences of their actions. This should not be seen as a fatalistic viewpoint and should not lead to inaction on our part. We must do all that we can to look after our own well-being and not suffer passively by remedying the situation. The same applies to good things as well; no one can help us unless we deserve it, but that shouldn't stop us from feeling grateful to the person as they deserve the credit for their intention to do good to us.

Loneliness

It is strange that this world is full of billions of people, but still, people feel lonely. Wherever we go we are part of a big crowd or a queue. Most public service departments cannot cope with the workload, be it police, social services, hospitals, transport, housing, etc. In existential terms loneliness is about not being able to open our hearts to someone and form lasting bonds. Nature has made each of us so different from each other that it's difficult to find someone you can connect with at a deeper level. If you have found such people, they should be taken very seriously and given top priority in our lives.

Loneliness does not just happen when we are alone; even those who live in a household full of people and a busy neighbourhood can feel lonely.

Every relationship has its own boundaries and beyond those boundaries we are all alone. Cynics would say that relationships act as a soothing balm that provides temporary relief from the loneliness that is at the bottom of our being, but one can argue that relationships are one of the things that make life worth living.

There are two types of loneliness – clinical, which is about not having a good social life and can be remedied, and existential, which cannot be remedied as it is related to the basic human condition – that no one can understand us

100% and to some extent the gap between us and others is unbridgeable. Accepting this kind of loneliness helps us deal with the stress better.

Loneliness and solitude are about being alone, but the difference between the two is vast. If being alone brings on negative or unpleasant feelings it is loneliness, but if it enriches us or brings peace and tranquillity it is solitude. It is possible to convert one's loneliness into solitude.

Envy and false pride

We normally assume that it is the "have-nots" who feel envious of "those who have", but strangely, envy is a disease that affects people irrespective of how much they have. It is not uncommon to find people who, in our eyes, have got everything but still they feel envious of those who have got more.

There is something magical about things that we do not possess. We assume that we will be all right once we have those things; but as soon as we have them they lose their charm. The goal-posts change and very soon we are looking for something else. We fail to understand that this feeling of "a lack" is not about things that exist outside of ourselves but about who we are deep inside. From a philosophical perspective we are all born with a feeling that something is lacking; all our actions are directed towards filling this void. Sadly this feeling of lack will never go, no matter what we do, as this is an existential condition that is at the bottom of our being. Lacan, a French philosopher, describes this feeling of lack as resulting from decentring of our consciousness and it requires inner work rather than acquiring objects in the external world. Scriptures also tell us that this lack is about our inability to grow spiritually and it goes away completely only when we have attained enlightenment.

Envy results from comparisons that are partial and not total. We see in others only one or two attributes that we lack and feel envious, not realising that there are dozens of other things in their lives that we have not looked at. If we honestly did a full assessment of people's lives, we would have compassion and sympathetic joy rather than envy and false pride.

Feelings of envy are considered undesirable as they cause discomfort to the person who experiences them and can make them do things that could be morally wrong. The positive side of envy is that it can inspire us to do things that we would not have thought of otherwise.

Depression

Others can only ignore you, ill-treat you, want to harm you, say unpleasant things to you, but they can't force you to experience depression.

Do you see yourself as a victim of society? Or is it that you have allowed yourself to feel that way? You can start exploring how you have allowed others to make decisions for you and to control you.

Depression almost always occurs in the interpersonal context and depends on our understanding of our relatedness to the world. It could result from a lack of connectedness with the world. Being more engaged with the world can be the answer to this lack of connectedness.

Suicidal thoughts and self-harm ideas

> *"It is the hope of death that keeps me alive*
> *I shall go to my master soon.*
> *Where hunger and thirst, and piercing cold and raging heat will be no more*
> *No ruler to be dreaded, no informer to be feared*
> *No rent to be paid, no clothes to be bought*
> *No meat to be sent for, no bread to be baked*
> *The world of delight, the state of pure delight."*
>
> Ghalib (2003)

Wanting to die is an extreme form of unhappiness, but if you knew that extreme unhappiness and extreme happiness can sit side by side you wouldn't be desperate to end it all. Having suicidal thoughts does not rule out the possibility of happiness, as you might find that after a few hours or days you are having a good time, maybe at a party or in the company of friends and family.

Imagining your mind in terms of a sea bed, which has got all sorts of beautiful and horrible things in it, can be helpful. Just as we cannot wipe the sea bed clean similarly we cannot get rid of the negative forces in the unconscious mind (when we set out on this journey). In view of this understanding, if we let the suicidal and self-harm thoughts stay where they are and we go about having a good time, then this can be helpful. These suicidal thoughts will become feebler and feebler as you spend more and more time creating positive experiences.

The presence of suicidal thoughts has been linked with having low coping abilities. Having suicidal thoughts does not mean that you have exhausted your coping resources; it simply means that the strategies that you have learned so far are not working in this particular situation. It is important to understand the difference between the coping resources and the strategies. You might have enormous coping resources, but if you haven't learned enough strategies to manage your moods you might feel out of your depth in a given situation.

Some individuals have a romantic relationship with their suicidal thoughts, as if it were their beloved who would rescue them from all their problems. It goes with the thinking that the thought of death makes life more tolerable. It is like a fantasy land where they will be free from all the miseries of the world. After committing suicide they will be able to leave behind all the worries of this world. Unfortunately, the contrary is the case for the depressed individual, as depression is not the malady of the body that is left behind, but that of the consciousness that goes with them.

CHAPTER 5

Lifestyle and Stress

Everything that we do causes stress, but it gets worked on in the normal course, unless our natural ability to undo is impaired. It is easy to understand that doing too much can cause stress, but doing too little can also cause stress. If one has not realised one's potential to a reasonable extent, it can cause stress that comes with feelings of existential guilt.

Lifestyle can cause stress and changing it can result in recovery; there may not be any need for professional help if one can discover the links between one's symptoms and lifestyle, and has normal coping abilities.

I remember a client of mine who had suffered from anxiety associated with a number of physical symptoms, such as hyperacidity, tension headaches, tiredness, sleep problems, etc., and he reported a complete remission in his symptoms after attending just one therapy session, which involved a discussion on how his lifestyle was causing the symptoms.

Lifestyle can be understood in terms of a number of different aspects as described in the following sections.

Personality and stress

It is not difficult to understand that if we asked a poet to work as an accountant or a philosopher to fight a war, they would get stressed. It is therefore important to know one's own personality.

One man's meat is another man's poison. What is a coping mechanism for your friend might be a real stress for you. It is important to know what situations, people and things make you stressed and what helps you.

- Are you a reserved or a social person?
- Do you have an artistic or scientific mind?
- Are you a philosopher, rebel, warrior, teacher, preacher, healer, mystic, manager, worker, etc.?
- Do you like mathematics or music or philosophy?
- Do you prefer security over adventure? Do you stay within conventions or like being unconventional?

Answers to all these questions can help you understand why you get stressed doing certain tasks and in certain situations, and tailor your life in a way that reduces your stress and enhances your life satisfaction.

At the simplest level there are two types of people: introverts and extroverts. It is not uncommon to see introverts being jealous of extroverts and vice versa. The extroverts make friends very easily and appear very confident in social situations, making the introverts want to become like them.

However, the downside of being an extrovert is that they make enemies also too easily and have difficulty bringing intensity in their work. Introverts, on the other hand, have fewer enemies and they can be more focused in their work, the qualities extroverts want. This could be a source of stress as one struggles to imbibe the qualities of the other. The solution to this problem lies in an introvert trying to be a successful introvert and in an extrovert being a successful extrovert, by way of playing on their own strengths.

The second aspect worth mentioning here is that an introvert's batteries are charged in solitude whereas an extrovert finds social situations rejuvenating. This fact has important implications in coping with stress (i.e. introverts should find time for solitude at the end of a hectic day and extroverts should have social avenues available to them after finishing work).

Assagioli (1986), an Italian therapist who pioneered a treatment approach called psychosynthesis, developed four different questionnaires for different age group clients to help the therapist understand the personalities of their clients whilst treating them. Most of the following questions are taken from his questionnaires.

- Who is your ideal person? And what do you admire most in them and why?
- What kinds of books/songs do you like most? Which books have caused you harm and why?
- Which films have impressed you most?
- If you had a great deal of money how would you spend it?
- What significance and value has friendship for you?
- How do you distinguish good from evil?
- Which studies and activities do you prefer most?
- How do you see yourself in five years' time?
- What are the factors limiting your psychological growth?
- Do you prefer to be in the country, at the sea or in a town/city?
- What is your attitude towards love? What do you think of the opposite sex?
- What events and what inner conditions make, or have made, you suffer most?
- What events and what inner conditions give, or have given, you the greatest joy? In what situations/activities do you get your peak experiences?
- What do you think of the present political and economic conditions of the world?

According to the Jungian psychology (1959) every man has a feminine side and every woman has a masculine side to them. Life could become richer and more complete if men developed the feminine side of their psyche and women their masculine. I am not suggesting that men should adopt feminine roles and women masculine, but to acquire the sensitivity to be able to look at this world and appreciate things from each other's perspective.

Nietzsche (1883) argued that man has to go through the ordeal of the three metamorphoses, through which the spirit will become a camel, a lion, and then a child. The spirit as camel will not refuse anything that needs to be borne, but will bear it, no matter how heavy. The next step (i.e. spirit of a lion) captures freedom in order to rule and be independent of duty. The final stage is that of a child, of innocence and forgetfulness, a new beginning and a "sacred Yes" (Deurzen, 1997).

Work and stress

For the majority of us, work is a means to something and not an end in itself. We tend to fantasise about a time when we will have plenty of money so that we won't have to work. Some individuals work harder than others so that they can afford to retire earlier. This supports the assumption that the desire not to work is stronger than the desire to work.

Imagine a hypothetical situation where your salary was guaranteed to you whether you came to work or not, would you still work? If your answer to this question is "No" it means your work, its nature or amount, might be depleting you in some ways. You need to ask yourself what you like about your work – the process (the actual work) or the outcome. If you find that you do not enjoy the actions that you carry out, you are missing the noble part of your job.

The common causes of work-related stresses are:

- Physical environment
- Travel, long hours, shift work
- Authoritarian superiors
- Colleagues with abrasive personalities can cause stress by ignoring the interpersonal aspects of feelings and sensibilities within social interaction
- Job insecurity
- Work overload/under-load
- New technology
- Role ambiguity/conflict
- Mismatch of formal and actual powers
- Difficult subordinates/colleagues

Symptoms of work-related stress

- Individual symptoms: irritability, depression, hypertension, chest pain, smoking, excessive drinking, etc.
- Organisational symptoms: high absenteeism, high staff turnover, poor quality control, etc.

The solution to this problem is simple – either you change your job or change your attitude to it. There is a third way as well – doing your job differently (i.e. making your work that you do loveable). You can say the following to yourself:

- I chose this job and I am willing to face the consequences of it. I am free to leave it whenever I want as I am not a bonded labourer. If my job is not making me happy I am not going to stay in it permanently; I will leave it when it is wise to do so, until then I will try the following things.
- There is more to work than the jobs that need doing.
- Good and bad people are equally distributed in this world. If I do not feel connected with people at my workplace and neighbourhood there is little chance it will happen elsewhere.
- Communicating with everyone at an adult to adult level rather than being a child in front of the authority figures and/or a parent with subordinates.
- Doing work as if it was my personal job.
- Taking short breaks: micro, mini and mega.
- Knowing your colleagues better, being interested in people and their lives without being too intrusive.
- Having the courage to voice one's disagreements openly.
- Making efforts to have a "life after five".
- Creating alternative sources of pleasure.

Choosing the work that suits your intelligence type

Your work should offer you the opportunity to do what you are best at doing and in this respect it's best to know your personality, type of intelligence and potentials.

Until recently it was believed that intelligence was a single entity and can be captured by a single number. However, a number of investigators have put forth the view that the mind consists of several independent modules or intelligences. Howard Gardner (1983) has proposed a theory of multiple intelligences and has argued for the following seven different types of intelligence. Each type of intelligence has its own strengths and constraints and would be suitable for certain types of vocation.

- Linguistic intelligence: poets, lawyers, speakers
- Logical-mathematical intelligence: scientists, mathematicians
- Musical intelligence: composers, singers
- Spatial intelligence: sculptor, airplane pilot, architects
- Bodily-kinetic intelligence: athlete, dancer
- Interpersonal intelligence: salesman, teacher, political leaders, educators, counsellors
- Intrapersonal intelligence: mystic, meditator, priest

You can choose your vocation depending upon your type of intelligence and by doing so you will be playing on your strengths and not weaknesses.

Leisure and recreation

Holidays are always the time we look forward to and imagine that all stress will be gone once we reach our destination. Holidays are times to create positive memories that will nourish us all our lives; they are about sharing good times with our loved ones.

It does work for many, but for some stress follows them on holidays as a trailer attached to a car. Long waits at the airports could be more tiring than the routine office and housework. The food and the hotel rooms may not be as good as at home. Lying on beautiful sandy beaches could be relaxing, but it can cause sunburn, skin allergies and mosquito bites to some, which will take days to heal. For some, holiday schedules are more hectic than their routine life and they come back to work for relaxation. Holidays may not help if one hasn't learnt how to undo stress and relax.

Quite often during holiday time you start asking the existential questions that you normally put aside as there is no time for them in your busy daily life; questions such as – Where am I going? What have I achieved in life so far? Is it worth all the effort that has gone in? What is the purpose of life? Life after retirement and old age? And the biggest of all questions – What about death?

Sometimes problems in a relationship surface during holiday periods when there are no distractions from one's inner resentments and anger. When one is freed from the constraints of daily routine, certain deeper, less pressing and hitherto ignored issues may become more apparent. In order to avoid this situation many couples plan holidays with other couples so that the deeper issues of the relationship will not emerge.

The need for a break: I see many clients who find it difficult to work non-stop for more than a few months without wanting a break and are desperate for a holiday. This situation arises if we haven't created enough short breaks in our daily life. Is it not a good idea to build little pockets of relaxation in one's everyday life?

Food and stress

We shouldn't eat just for our tongue but for the whole body. In certain Eastern cultures they discourage people from chasing the pleasures of tasty food. Normally eating is a response to certain outer and inner signals, including hunger. The sources of these signals could be as follows:

- Tongue: which makes you want to eat only the tastiest food.
- Mind: when you start counting calories and ingredients in each food item (i.e. presence of essential ingredients, vitamins, trace elements, etc.).
- Gut/body: when your biological hunger and other inner signals dictate the nature and quantity of food.
- Clock: when you want to eat just because it's time to eat and not eating can create problems for you.
- External signals: from parents, carers, authorities, menu, etc.

We can get the following two types of signals from each of the above sources:

- Yes, go ahead and eat.
- No, do not eat.

It may be that the signals that we receive from the above sources differ from each other and create conflicts within us. For example, when taking a bitter medicine the tongue says "no", but the mind says "yes". The gut remains neutral here as the medicine is not perceived as a need by the body unless one is familiar with the effect it has on one's feeling state. When the tongue wins we decide not to take the medicine and take it when the mind wins.

The most important of all the above sources and the one that should be respected most is the signal from the gut/body. Unfortunately, quite often we fail to perceive this signal as a result of being disconnected from our bodies and choosing to be guided by our tongue and other signals.

Our perception of these signals depends a lot on the level of consciousness that we are in at a given point in time. We get partially cut off from the gut signals under stressful conditions or when we are engaged in other activities, such as watching television while eating. The "stop" signal coming from our body whilst eating gets ignored as a result and in the absence of the inner signals we are governed by the tongue signal that results in overeating.

In order to stay connected with one's body one can shift the attention from thoughts to perception (i.e. focusing intensely on the smell of food, its colour, its texture when it touches lips and tongue). This extra focus on sensation can also help in digestion. The food should be chewed properly and the pace of eating should not be fast. There are certain body-mind therapies, such as mindfulness meditation, that can help you stay connected with your own body and modulate your hunger.

The role of fasting

Apart from the religious reasons there are good reasons to go on short periods of fasting or skipping meals. However, it may not be a good idea to skip breakfast if you feel hungry mid-morning as it can cause a dip in your energy levels.

It is not difficult to understand that an average person in an average day eats more than they should and this needs to be compensated in some way. Fasting could be an answer to this problem. There are two types of fasting – natural and forced. Eventually the fasting should become natural as prolonged periods of disciplined fasting can be harmful.

The role of taste

Taste in food is a relative term. What appears very tasty at the start of the meal might make us feel sick if we go on eating it. A starving person can tell you how delicious a dry piece of bread is.

On a hungry stomach we can find most edible things tasty. If you can enjoy only a very limited range of good stuff it may be that you are not allowing yourself to experience hunger properly. If you try eating things that you normally do not like after a period of starvation you will be surprised to learn how delicious they are.

We can divide the tasty food into two categories: the naturally tasty food and the one that was made tasty artificially. Taking more of what you find naturally tasty is better than the tasty meal seen on the restaurant menu. Wanting to eat tasty food at each mealtime and being guided entirely by taste can be a recipe for health problems.

Having a second (late night) meal

If you are working late at night it seems reasonable to snack, but if it makes you feel full in the morning and skip your breakfast, it may not be healthy as you might feel hungry mid-morning the next day.

Obesity and stress

Is obesity a disease, an unhealthy lifestyle issue or just a normal variation? The answer could be yes to all these options. We have seen the definition of obesity changing in the last few years. What was considered overweight ten years ago is now considered normal weight and what was treated as obesity in the past is now just overweight.

It would be wrong to hold everyone who is obese responsible for their weight. Some are obese as a result of their actions whereas others are obese in spite of all their actions. I have seen obese people who are much more disciplined and have a greater sense of self-control compared to so-called normal weight people. It is unfortunate that all obese people are treated in the same fashion and health professionals have been reluctant to treat illnesses that go with obesity.

For some obese individuals stress plays an important role. Stress can work in two different ways: it can disrupt the individual's connection with their inner state of affairs or/and they are trying to manage their stress by way of eating. Helping a client pick up the inner cues of stress/discomfort and working on them at the mental level can reduce the need to eat.

Coping strategy: To learn a relaxation therapy that is consistent with your physiology and practise it when upset rather than reaching out for food. The golden rule is not to eat when upset – give yourself about fifteen minutes during which time you can practise some form of relaxation and eat after this exercise in "the mindful way".

Body-mind therapies, such as Vipassana meditation (discussed in the spirituality section of this book), can help clients stay connected with their bodies and bring about the desired results.

Small tips for eating healthily

- Leaving about one fourth of your stomach empty when you finish your meal.
- Eating more frequently, i.e. taking small snacks (one fruit or ten cashew nuts or other equivalent dry fruits) every three/four hours and making the main meal smaller.
- Trying different experiments with your diet – including more vegetarian ingredients and raw uncooked food.
- Drinking more water. If you don't like to drink water try distilled water, as some find it more compatible with their gastrointestinal system, or flavoured water.
- The discomfort that makes us eat may be about other things (i.e. not having enough fresh air, thirst, sitting in one posture for too long, not taking adequate breaks when working, mental conflict, etc.).

- Our bodies have the ability to detoxify wrong food within limits. Detox diets become necessary if we have been overeating and using high calorie food for several days on end.
- Intense mental work also consumes energy and creates hunger – there is no harm in supplying extra calories to the brain at these times to increase the capacity of the mind to manage the task at hand – you can always compensate for it later on.
- At times it is not the calorie requirement but the stomach acid that makes us eat more – it's best to eat a piece of bread to absorb the acid rather than eat a proper snack or meal. Cutting down on tea, coffee, late night meals, spicy foods, smoking and practising relaxation sessions can help us deal with hyperacidity.
- Not eating a balanced meal keeps the hunger signal on even after we have eaten sufficient quantity as the body needs those ingredients that are not there in the meal you have given to it.

Sleep – an antidote to stress

"And when night comes I take good care not to summon Sleep! He, the lord of virtues, does not like to be summoned!"

Nietzsche (1983)

There are three types of sleep patterns:

- Long: more than nine hours per day
- Average: between seven and nine hours
- Short: less than seven hours

If you know your normal sleep requirement you won't struggle too much trying to control it.

Emmy van Deurzen[1] (1997) has described the following formula given by Nietzsche for a healthy living:

- We must aim to overcome ourselves ten times a day; exhausting our energies and living to the full in the process.

- We must ten times also reconcile ourselves with ourselves, for bitterness is a bad way to be and stops us sleeping at night.
- We must also discover ten truths a day, in order to quench our thirst for truth.
- Finally, we must laugh and be cheerful ten times a day, as the wisdom that brings no laughter is false.

She further quotes Nietzsche, "Whilst waiting for sleep, I remember what I have done and thought during the day. Ruminating I ask myself, patient as a cow: what were your ten over-comings? And which were the ten reconciliations and the ten truths and the ten fits of laughter with which my heart enjoyed itself. By the time you complete this exercise you might be fast asleep." (Deurzen, 1997)

Sleep can also be understood with the help of the analogy of a bus that comes at regular intervals to the bus stop. If you have missed one, you need to wait until the next one arrives. But if you leave the bus stop (i.e. get up from your bed and start doing things) you might miss the next bus as well. Being awake in bed at night is the best time to practise relaxation exercises and also to plan your day ahead.

> *"O sleep! O gentle sleep!*
> *Nature's soft nurse, how have I frightened thee.*
> *That thou no more wilt weigh my eyelids down*
> *And steep my senses in forgetfulness?"*
>
> William Shakespeare (1992)

Relationships and Stress: Cause or Cure?

Children and stress

It is stressful not to have children and to have children is also stressful, but it's better to have children and face the stress than have no children. We are not perfect parents and therefore do not deserve perfect children. Children who are born in our families do not deserve better parents otherwise they would have been born somewhere else. Similarly, we do not deserve better children than the ones we have got. If that were the case, we would have got a different set of children.

Many clients come and ask me why their teenage kids behave strangely and do things that are totally out of character for them. For many children it's about shopping around for an identity; they want to try out different ways of being before they settle for the kind of person they want to be. It's like when we go to the market to buy something; we don't just go to the first shop and buy a product. We make enquiries about the price and the quality of the product from several shops before settling for a product. It's okay for children to try out different ways of being within safe and reasonable limits as long as the consequences of their actions are not irreversible, such as teenage pregnancies.

Parents and stress

Parents are the greatest source of comfort for a child; gradually as one grows up they become less important and eventually they can become a source of stress in their old age.

Children tend to have idealised views of their parents:

- My mum is the most beautiful woman in the world; she is the best cook.
- My dad is the best employee at his workplace; he is very strong.

This results from having no opportunity to compare their parents with others or not having the ability to do so in a mature fashion. Gradually as we gain this ability we start seeing imperfections in our parents. Out of love for them we try to make up for their deficiencies by trying to include those qualities in us that we think are lacking in our parents.

We often see that children try to finish the unfinished business of their parents and want to be successful in pursuits that their parents struggled with. Sometimes it's just the opposite when one identifies negatively with their parents. They don't want to repeat the mistakes of their parents and do just the opposite. However, this could be a trap as there is a small possibility that in trying to avoid the mistakes of their parents they end up repeating the mistakes of their grandparents (assuming that their parents did the same when they were young).

In childhood we identify with our parents, in adulthood with our partners and in old age with our children. These relationships can become symbolic of how we relate to this world. Conflicts in this network of relationship can affect us at a much deeper level than we generally appreciate, as these bonds are generally deeper than we assume them to be.

In order to make a healthy start of adult life it is important not to carry the emotional baggage of our adolescent years. We can make a beginning in this regard by forgiving our parents for all their perceived failures and mistakes.

Social life

Nobody is as good or as bad as we imagine them to be.

There are two types of anxieties worth mentioning here: separation anxiety and engulfment anxiety. Relationships can be a source of stress and at the same time they can relieve stress.

These two opposing views can be explained further taking examples from the writings of two philosophers: Jean-Paul Sartre and Martin Buber. Sartre's (1944) famous quote "hell is other people" suggests that we lose authenticity when we enter into a relationship; we lose a bit of ourselves in trying to relate to others. Whereas, Martin Buber (1923), a German philosopher, talked about the sacredness of every human relationship – that we grow only through our contact and relatedness to other human beings. Buber talked about two different kinds of relationships: *I-It* and *I-Thou*. The *I-It* relationship is characterised by treating others as things and using them for one's selfish purposes, whereas the *I-Thou* relationship is about enjoying being with other human beings without expecting anything from them. It may be that we lose authenticity when we enter into *I-It* relationships and gain authenticity by entering into *I-Thou* relationships.

Buber spoke eloquently about "in-between" in relationships and described it as "when I do not rob you of your space and you do not rob me of mine, a new, more open, space between us is created and in this we can generate interaction. I no longer have to strive to defend myself from being altered by you. I no longer have to aim for altering you; I can safely venture forward towards the new space that we inhabit together and I can meet you there in order to weave a new world out of what we both have to offer" (quoted in Emmay van Deurzen, 1997).

It would be easier for us to manage the stresses related to our relationships if we could convert our *I-It* relationships into *I-Thou* relationships.

Time management

If you have a dozen pending bills to pay, a flight and a hotel to book for attending a conference next week, a talk to prepare for tomorrow's meeting, kids to be picked up from school in the next hour, a doctor's appointment for ECG, your mum to be taken shopping, twenty-four emails to be answered and you can't say "no" to people who expect you to do things that you do not want to do, how can you relax? The demands on your time do not become less by themselves; something has to be done.

The demands on time and energy are multiple and unending. Stress results when you feel that you have lost control over your daily schedule and have little time in which to attend to your own needs.

Time management methods are designed to help individuals restore a sense of balance in their lives. The programme includes:

- The client gaining an enhanced awareness of the current pattern of time used by keeping a record of how they spend their time each day.
- Amount of time they would like to spend in each activity.
- Setting priorities in terms of urgency and importance as follows:

Urgent Non-Important Activities 1....... 2.......	Urgent Important Activities 1....... 2.......
Non-Urgent Non-Important Activities 1....... 2.......	Non-Urgent Important Activities 1....... 2.......

Clients might realise that they are spending too much time on urgent but non-important tasks and ignoring non-urgent but important tasks.

- Goal-setting and being more focused on specific behaviour change targets that fit with an individual's immediate and long-term goals.
- Dealing with procrastination can prevent stress.
- Planning to arrive at least five or ten minutes in advance for each appointment can help prevent a lot of stress resulting from running late.
- The proverb "A stitch in time saves nine" can be applied to a lot of things that, if done in time, can *save* time, effort and energy eventually.

Energy Management

The concept of energy management is new in the field of stress management. It relates to paying attention to and managing everything that impacts on one's level of energy. It may be true that some people are born with very high levels of energy, which enables them to accomplish extraordinary tasks without any conscious effort. But for the majority of us, careful planning and efforts can result in high levels of energy. Energy can be conceptualised as the fuel that propels the engine of our life at three different levels. These three levels can also be seen as the sources of energy.

- ➤ Physical energy: the energy for physical activity comes from the food that we eat, our genetic disposition and the environment we live in.
- ➤ Mental energy.
- ➤ Spiritual energy.

Factors that deplete our energy:

- Eating – too much, wrong kind of food and at wrong times
- Skipping meals and crash dieting
- Negative emotions, poor stress tolerance
- Relationship problems at work and in personal life
- Being in the company of a stress-prone person
- Inherent dislike for the task ahead

- Too much pending work
- Negative environmental condition
- Disapproval of others and antagonism
- Hot climate
- Sleep deprivation

Factors that boost our energy:

- High achievement motivation
- Seeing purpose and meaning in the task at hand
- The tasks are in keeping with one's life goals and aptitude
- Successful completion of a task
- Approval of peer and seniors
- Harmony in relationships
- Hopefulness
- Music and other relaxation techniques
- Being in the company of people with good auras
- Meditation, prayers
- Feeling connected spiritually

Clients are encouraged to make a list of their energy-depleting and energy-boosting situations and use it in planning activities.

Enjoying old age

"I wish I was twenty years younger; hold on, I am twenty years younger."

I recently met a friend of mine who was fifty-eight and chose to retire. He told me, "I wish I was twenty years younger; I could have done a lot more, but now my life seems to have gone past me. I must quietly retire and take a back seat. There is no need to struggle too much."

I said to him, "I met someone last week who was seventy-eight and he said exactly the same words, 'I wish I was twenty years younger; at fifty-eight I was in good health and full of energy, free from house mortgage, financially secure, no responsibilities of children, able to travel around, start a new venture, grow professionally, spiritually, socially, personally without any pressures on me'."

The problem is, when looking back most of us want to go back in time to recapture youthfulness but still keep what we have acquired in the intervening years. I imagined a fairy offering me the option of becoming twenty years younger on the condition that I would have to let go of everything I have acquired or become in the last twenty years, and I turned down the offer.

Old age conjures up images of people who are sick, frail and dependent on others. Elderly people are considered to be difficult, rigid, depressed, lonely, not able to cope well and cognitively impaired. Contrary to this, for most elderly people the debility is not severe enough to make enjoyment difficult. The majority find their current level of stress tolerable; in fact, they even tend to deny or underplay them. It's mainly the thoughts of the future, if they are not careful, that make some of them incapable of living in the present.

For some, old age is more like fatigue, except that they cannot correct it by relaxing or taking a vacation. This fatigue is probably more mental than physical as it has so little in common with the fatigue that follows physical labour (Skinner and Vaughan, 1983). The signs of this fatigue could be – feeling sorry for oneself, putting off decisions, unwilling to take exercise or relax, eating either too much or not enough, desire to lie in bed, use of improper language, etc.

The natural physical wear and tear that comes with advancing age is unavoidable, but the same law does not apply to the intellect and consciousness.

One can experience progressive clarity of thought with advancing age. Old age has its own compensations in terms of wisdom, equanimity, greater social contacts, social skills, less interpersonal inhibitions and worries about opinions of others.

Many elderly people describe their sixties as the best period of their lives, as they are more experienced in worldly things, free from the constraints of work, reasonably healthy, financially secure, mobile and physically capable.

However, there are specific worries related to old age, such as loss of friends, loneliness and preoccupation with death. Talking about death is an important aspect of coping for the elderly, but unfortunately, when they want to discuss this matter in the family, their children shut them up with remarks such as, "Dad, you are not going to die soon. Why then talk about it? Are you trying to gain sympathy?"

Sogyal Rinpoche (1992) has described the example of a woman in a hospice dying of breast cancer. Her daughter would visit her every day and there seemed to be a happy relationship between the two. But when her daughter had left, she would nearly always sit alone and cry. After a while it became clear that the reason for this was that her daughter had refused to accept the inevitability of her death, but spent her whole time encouraging her mother to "think positively", hoping that by doing this her cancer would be cured. All that happened was that the old woman had to keep her thoughts, deep fears, panic and grief to herself, with no one to share them with, no one to help her explore them, no one to help her understand her life and no one to help her find a healing meaning in her death.

The nature of stress in old age

Feeling useless and a burden: In old times grandparents played an important role in transmitting knowledge to children, which is now done by the internet. The counselling and career advice is nowadays sought from the career counsellors rather than elderly people. The bond between generations has become weaker with the state taking the responsibility to look after the elderly.

I often ask my elderly clients if they thought their children were a burden to them when they brought them up and the standard answer I get is, "No, not at all, it was a pleasure", and it's rare to find a child who feels guilty receiving care from his/her parents. However, when it comes to receiving care from children, most parents don't feel that way. They feel a sense of guilt when they have to become dependent on their children. They fail to see that their children are returning a debt owed to them.

There are some cultural differences here; I find that this guilt and the feeling of being a burden or a useless person is seen less often in the Asian cultures compared with the Western. The Asian parents, on the contrary, become resentful and unhappy if they do not receive proper care and attention from their offspring.

Boredom. Some see retirement as an escape, but soon realise that they have escaped from much that they actually liked. Their work took them out of the house, brought them in contact with other people and took up time that hangs heavily on their hands. They find that it is not "sweet to do nothing" for the rest of their lives (Skinner, 1983).

Feeling guilty because you are idle. To keep busy just because you feel you should is not likely to help. Instead of trying hard to enjoy what you are doing, try hard to find something you like better.

Anger and fear. Anger and frustration result from failure to do things properly.

Change of routine. Retirement could mean a change of place of residence, closer to children, moving into a smaller house, change of neighbourhood, loss of touch with local residents/friends, etc.

Sex and old age. Skinner (1982) quotes Paul Tillich's statement that "pornography could be justified on the grounds that it extended sexuality into old age". As long as sex is on the mind there is no harm in enjoying its presence, but its fading away can also be seen as an opportunity to work more effectively on the spiritual side of one's life.

Ways of coping

Old age is rather like another country. You will enjoy more if you have prepared yourself before you go. For that you need to learn as much as possible about the new country (i.e. climate, people, language, history, etc.) (Skinner, 1982). For most people planning for old age only means financial security, but that is just one part of it.

Keeping in touch with the world. Simple awareness of the importance of renewing your contact with old friends, relatives and colleagues can be useful in using this coping mechanism. Technology offers new ways of connecting with people. I have come across many old people who are technophobes and refuse to use emails and text messaging. I say to them – don't give up before you have tried it; just devote one full day trying to learn it from someone and it will bring you closer to a whole lot of people. Connecting with old friends needs deliberate action.

Keeping busy. It would be wrong to assume that nothing much is happening in the lives of elderly people, which may be true from the point of view of a working person. But the truth is that the elderly are much more connected with their community, politics of their family and social life. They are better informed about their relatives, neighbours, what's on television, the different soaps, prices of things in the superstore, etc. Their mental life is as rich as anybody else's. It's therefore not difficult for the elderly to keep busy if they want to.

Changing habits. Doing something different – reading a different paper, watching TV programmes that you once condemned as trash, using a different superstore for shopping or speaking to your neighbour you dismissed long ago as superficial and phony can be a stimulating experience.

Care of the house. The sheer care of the house can become a burden. It would be helpful if you tried getting rid of everything that you do not need. If possible, it is better to give special things to the special people now that you were going to leave them. Thoreau reportedly said that a man does not own a house, the house owns the man (Skinner, 1983).

Dealing with young people. Not letting younger people learn from their mistakes, reacting emotionally to their actions, wanting to spend too much time with younger people and not acting one's age can all lead to some stress.

Legal issues. Writing an advance directive about the care you want to receive in the hospital, whether you would like to be resuscitated, given a particular treatment, etc. can reduce some of your worries about the future. A properly executable will might give you the satisfaction of knowing that your possessions will go to the right people.

Death: Is it a catastrophe?

> *"Men come and they go and they trot and they dance, never a word about death; all well and good. Yet when death does come – to them, their wives, their children, their friends – catching them unawares and unprepared then what storms of passion overwhelm them, what cries, what fury, what despair.*

> *To begin depriving death of its greatest advantage over us, let us adopt a way clean contrary to that common one; let us deprive death of its strangeness, let us frequent it, let us get used to it; let us have nothing more often in mind than death… we do not know where death awaits us; so let us wait for it everywhere. To practise death is to practise freedom. A man who has learned how to die has unlearned how to be a slave."*

> Montaigne (1991)

A life well lived prepares us to accept death and the thoughts of death prepare us to live better. It is the richness and completeness of one's life experiences that make one embrace death.

People who live with the feeling that life has passed them by find it difficult to die and are constantly worried about getting old and aging. They are always trying to be smarter and better than their fellow individuals, seeking more of worldly success and sense pleasure, which in some situations may be a defence against one's death anxiety.

Death anxiety is the mother of all anxieties. Death is a taboo subject maybe because of the assumption that we will end up feeling worse thinking about it, and thinking about it is not going to help anyway. Strangely the truth is just the opposite. Thinking about death may not make us wiser about death or make us see what is on the other side of death, but it can certainly make us less scared of it and enhance our happiness of life. People who live constantly with thoughts of their mortality are able to engage in things that truly matter and as a result enrich their lives. However, thinking about death may not be advisable for people who experience unbearable anxiety at the thought of death and are unable to work with it.

In some religious sects, frequent reminders of our mortality is considered helpful. Simply dwelling on death doesn't bring it forward; on the contrary it makes us enjoy life more as life looks so much more beautiful in contrast.

Death is not something that will happen one fine day in the distant future. If we examine our lives very closely we are changing every minute and moving closer to death – we are dying every minute and this realisation can make us enjoy life more and be less fearful of death.

CHAPTER 6

Love, Sex and Relationships

"It is not for the sake of the husband [or the wife] that the husband is loved, but for the sake of the Self that the husband is loved."
Brihadaranyaka Upanishad (1983)

If you think you haven't found true love or the right partner there is no need to worry too much; you are in the majority. It is my rough estimate that about 60% of the general population live with the thought that they haven't found true love or the right partner; another 20% suffer from delusion of love (i.e. believe they have found true love when they haven't) and it's only the remaining 20% who have truly found their soul mates and would still want to be with the same partner in their next life, if there is one.

You can't create the magic of love, nor can you make it disappear instantly. You can't choose to fall in love or fall out of it by will. It just happens to you. You can only create conditions to increase its likelihood of happening or fading away, but the results are not guaranteed.

However, you can certainly do the following:

- Make your love grow and mature
- Slowly destroy or cripple it
- Not see when it's there
- Imagine that it's there when it is not
- Know it's not real although in the beginning you thought it was
- Know it's real now although you first thought it wasn't

What is love?

It's a very straightforward question, but the answer is not that easy. There are couples who can't live without each other, but who still don't see the other person as their soul mate, and there are couples who can't live together, but who still see each other as their soul mate. There are individuals who have great physical and psychological intimacy, but who are still searching, and there are individuals who feel unfulfilled, but who consider themselves settled in relationships.

It's difficult to decide the core ingredients of true love – is it physical intimacy, friendship, companionship, commitment, fulfilment, exclusivity and being faithful or is it something more? – in the realms of spiritual or divine connections.

How to know whether you are truly in love or whether it's just infatuation? Reflection on the following might help:

- When you have butterfly feelings and feel on cloud nine all the time
- When you become obsessed with the person and can't free your mind
- When you want to spend the rest of your life with that person
- When the person makes you feel very special
- When you know that the person is completely honest and genuine with you and you want to be the same
- When you put the needs of your beloved above your needs or on a level with your needs
- When you want to be with the same person in your next life as well, if you believe in rebirth

Types of love:

1. **Self-gratifying love**: The person who is in love is thinking about only their own needs and not those of the loved one. This can also be described as selfish love. It can be subdivided into several categories.

   A. **Beautiful love/puppy love:** The individual loves the act of falling in love with someone. It doesn't matter who this person is, nor their attributes. This is commonly seen in teenagers who have never been in love and are desperate to have this experience.

   B. **Honey type of love**: The person is attracted to certain attributes that the other person holds; the emphasis again is on what they can get from the other person rather than what they are giving in the relationship. The love ends when the imagined or actual attributes that attracted in the first place are missing.

   C. **Heroic love:** Generally seen in men who can go to any length to protect and support their loved ones. They can fight wars, leave their jobs, friends and relatives for the sake of love, but will not do the little things that their partners need or want. They will not be good at looking after their loved ones when they are unwell.

2. **Self-sacrificing love**: It is also described as melting butter type of love, wherein the person sacrifices their self-interests to support their loved ones. It is unhealthy for the individual as there may be an element of being abused or exploited by the other person.

3. **Balanced love:** When one is able to strike a balance between what they are giving and what they are getting. This type of love is mutually rewarding, but it can run into problems if there is an imbalance in the give–get equation.

4. **Mature:** Love matures when the connection is deep and this type of love is irreversible. A break in the relationship is never right once the love matures as it will never fade, not even after the death of the person. The identities of the two persons are unified and the individual is happy to put the needs of the other person above their own needs. The cost–benefit analysis, as to who is giving and getting how much goes out of the equation.

5. **Love of a leader:** It's the love for one's clan, community and nation. It goes beyond one's family and friends. The individual identifies with a group of people and their needs become more important than their own needs.

6. **Spiritual love:** It is the ultimate expression of the self's deepest desire and its tendencies towards its source. It is universal and it can cross national and racial boundaries. The person sees every other human being, even animals, in the same way as a mother sees her own children. Just as a mother thinks that she owes something to the child all the time, similarly a spiritual person has this constant feeling that they owe something to humanity. Unfortunately, this and the love of a leader can create conflicts within the family if the family members do not understand it properly. They feel let down and begin to feel that what belongs to them is being distributed freely to all and sundry. A typical example of this in modern times is that of Nelson Mandela who was forced to choose between his marriage and his political life.

This classification can help clients understand the true nature of their love and take it to a mature level thereby minimising their life stress.

Sex and stress

The sexual drive, like any other, is in itself neither "bad" nor "good". In its original form it's pre-moral and not immoral, but individuals view it in quite opposite ways depending upon their own cultural and social learning. It is unfortunate that nature has given men and women two different sets of priorities and still created such a need for each other that they cannot live without the other.

Romantic and sexual feelings could be sublime as they give to some individuals the peak experiences of their life. Unfortunately, when it comes to these feelings our minds are generally ahead of our bodies and the outside reality. The mind doesn't stop having these thoughts even when our bodies are sending clear *no* signals, hence there is a need to work on these feelings.

Again there are gender differences here; generally for women the romantic feelings and the relationship are more important and sex should happen within the context of these things, whereas for men the physical aspects of the act can be an end in itself. To put it simply, for most women the relationship aspects are more important than the physical aspects and the reverse seems to be the case for men. In this respect I would say that women are more sensible than men as being in a relationship brings about satisfaction at a deeper level compared to the physicality of love-making. It is a different question whether women are able to satisfy their relationship needs or not, because at the end of the day those experiences have to come from men who may not be that sensitive in this area. One can argue for a similar case for men as well, as they are also in a similar situation.

Preconceived notions about what is normal in sex can cause some stress as it's a normal tendency to judge oneself in terms of the norms in the society. There is no such thing as normal sexual requirement – for some couples having sex three times a week is the norm whereas for others once in a year is perfectly normal.

Sex and clinical anxiety

Anxiety and sex are each other's enemies. Anxiety impairs sexual desire and performance and sexual activity can lead to a dramatic reduction in one's anxiety levels. There is a gender difference here; men report more ejaculatory and erection problems under stress, whereas women suffer from low sexual desire under stress. That is not to say all women who have low desire are suffering from stress. Spiritually inclined individuals can have low sexual desire coupled with a higher sense of well-being.

Teenage sex

It appears to be a feature of the modern times that some teenagers enter into relationships as soon as they attain the physical maturity to have sexual experience. At times they start a relationship as a result of peer pressure even though they themselves do not feel the need for one. As a result they do not always get the opportunity to learn to handle their sexuality and the need for companionship outside physical relationships. They need another relationship as soon as one ends as they haven't acquired the skills to be on their own. This inability can result in disastrous consequences as one can't wait to make informed and well thought out choices. It would be advisable not to be in a relationship for at least a few years after attaining puberty so that one learns to handle the desire for sexual experience without succumbing to it.

Sex in marriage

Early on in history there was no such thing as marriage. Men and women, as in the case of animals, mated promiscuously. The institution of marriage has been viewed as the outcome of experimentation with a number of different arrangements, but in the modern world it seems to be on shaky ground.

Marriage should signify a union of hearts between the two partners and sex is seen as an essential ingredient of a good marriage. A good marriage conjures up images of a good sex life, but strangely in my clinical practice I have come across many couples who describe their marriage or relationship as very good, but their sex life "not all that good". For the majority of such couples, not having a reasonably satisfactory sex life could indicate problems, both medical or psychological, but for a small minority it could just be that they have outgrown this need and its absence does not affect the closeness of their relationship. On the contrary, they experience a more mature closeness as they are out of the sexual politics of the relationship. In fact, in certain cultures couples are encouraged to take their relationship to that level.

Sublimation of sexual tension

A gradual process of transmutation takes place normally and spontaneously in harmoniously married couples. At the beginning, the sexual and intensely emotional manifestations of love generally predominate, but in the course of years and decades this passionate aspect cools off and is transmuted into tender feelings, increasing mutual understanding, appreciation and inner communion. The transmutation of love can further expand to love for humanity and creative activities of an artistic or intellectual nature (Assagioli, 1984).

A switch of energy from sexual to creative pursuits is evident in Richard Wagner's life history. He chose to renounce the consummation of his love to Mathilde, a married woman to whom he gave music lessons and in whom he found an understanding of and a devotion to his genius. He left Zurich for Venice to get away from her and as a result became suicidal, but soon he set himself to write both the libretto and music of *Tristan and Isolde*, and in a kind of frenzy completed the opera within a few months. In his letters to Mathilde, one can see a gradual cooling off of his passion as he gave expression to it in the poetry and music of his opera (Assagioli, 1984).

Sexual activity (very much like music) can have totally different effects at different times depending upon the level of consciousness we are in. If we are feeling anxious and low, sex can have an elevating effect on our moods, but if we are already at a higher level of consciousness and experiencing inner peace and bliss it can pull us down to a normal level of consciousness. Just as the same piece of music can be soothing and sublime at one time and irritating at other times depending upon our moods.

CHAPTER 7

What Is Psychotherapy – And How Does It Work?

"What is the point in narrating the whole sad story to yet another therapist who is there just to listen? They can't change the reality of my life. It will bring back all the bad memories and I will end up feeling worse than how I am feeling now."

This is a common sentiment I come across during my psychiatric assessments. Perhaps the individual who says this is right, as they may not know how to deal with what is uncovered during therapy. Such individuals need to equip themselves with tools in coping with their stress before they undertake any exploratory work.

Research carried out in recent years on debriefing (narrating traumatic experiences to a professional colleague after experiencing a stressful event) supports the observation that debriefing can be both helpful and harmful. It seems that debriefing helps those who are able to process the negative experiences at their own pace and in a secure setting, but makes things worse for those who cannot manage the anxiety involved in relating the painful experience. If you belong to the second category you need to discuss issues of safety and timing with your therapist, so that together you can modify the therapeutic relationship and setting.

Counselling and psychotherapy have been used as a panacea for all psychological problems and there is a justification for doing so. Coming into contact with a caring and genuine human being who has received special training and has worked through their own inner stresses and mental conflict can be helpful. Unfortunately, there are so many who need psychotherapy and very few who can deliver the goods or are honest enough to admit to their clients that they cannot help. This creates a situation where the demand outstrips the supply. As a result many who can benefit from psychotherapy go without it. This problem can be solved only when psychotherapeutic principles move beyond the confines of professional settings and into mainstream life.

Formal versus informal forms of psychotherapy

Advice from a wise person, or careful listening from a friend, can bring about the same sort of results as formal psychotherapy, but there are differences between the two. It's important to decide whether formal psychotherapy is needed from professionals in a given situation or the problems can be tackled using either self-help techniques described in this book or making use of the informal systems of help from friends, relatives and the wider network of support in the community, including spiritual practices such as yoga and meditation.

Clients are well advised to take full responsibility to make use of the space in therapy by being active and bringing issues for discussions. What is in the unconscious will gradually come to the surface of the mind and get worked on. Sometimes clients discover new elements in their thinking for the first time when they are narrating their problems to the therapist. It's very much like thinking about your problems before going to bed so that your unconscious dreaming mind can act on them whilst you are still asleep. For many people this is a naturally occurring healing process, but for others their dreams will take the form of disturbing nightmares. Those of us who can dream happily probably do not need professional or formal psychotherapy. Those of us who are suffering from nightmares and flashbacks might do better to call in some additional help in the form of psychotherapy.

What heals in psychotherapy?

Several years ago I asked my teacher this question and his prompt reply was a relationship. I wasn't fully satisfied with this answer as I wanted to know what was in a therapeutic relationship that was not there in other relationships (i.e. with our spouse, relatives, friends and teachers). I asked for further clarification and his answer was that through the therapeutic relationship you are brought closer to "the reality". So it was about understanding "reality" in a more complete fashion, which is normally beyond us. It has something to do with getting honest and open feedback in a secure setting where feedback is a two-way process that is welcomed by the therapist as well as by the patient.

Our friends and family can offer feedback that will put us in touch with this "reality"; but their opinions are likely to be biased and may not have the same impact. Our friends are probably too kind to give us an honest opinion and may try to portray our weaknesses in a positive light. Our parents may have the need to maintain that they were good parents and the difficulties we feel we faced as children were somehow imaginary. This is an understandable thing given that for most of us quite a bit of our self-esteem is bound up with the idea of ourselves as caring, loving parents.

Therapy is an opportunity to get a less biased opinion on one's life situations. In essence, all psychotherapy can do is tell you what it's like for someone to be in a relationship with you and you should feel free to evaluate this feedback. Psychotherapists, like parents, will have their own prejudices and these may include wanting to portray themselves as therapists in a good light. However, a well-trained psychotherapist should be aware of these prejudices and should be able to talk to you about difficult aspects of the helping relationship, including ways in which you may feel distressed by the psychotherapy at times. Be wary of therapists who are not open to your comments about doubts or difficulties you are having early on with the psychotherapy process! However, well-conducted psychotherapy will give you the opportunity to look at past unresolved issues in a more objective way, informed by modern understanding of child development.

Another way of describing this involves talking about early attachments to our parents or first caretakers. About two-thirds of us make secure bonds with our parents. These are relationships where we feel our parents love and understand us. For this to happen our parents need to have been in a position where they can give most of their attention to looking after us as children. For about a third of us this situation did not occur and we never felt securely bonded to our parents. This insecure attachment gives rise to problems later on in life. Many people without secure attachments feel they cannot trust other people in relationships. As a result of this, they also feel they cannot trust themselves and they suffer from low self-esteem, anxiety and depression.

Children who are securely attached to their parents feel confident about leaving them behind and going out into the world to explore new environments and new relationships.

Children who are insecurely attached tend either to cling to their parents in an anxious way or to pretend that relationships don't matter at all and to become dependent upon things such as food or objects. Such people often go on in adult life to become addicted to drugs, alcohol or repetitive behaviours, such as cutting and overdosing when they are in emotional distress. They find it hard to turn to other people as a source of comfort, as quite naturally they have learnt to distrust people.

It is possible in psychotherapy to enter into a relationship with the therapist where some of these difficulties can be relived. By talking about the relationship you have with your therapist openly, you can explore the specific ways in which you feel misunderstood and the specific problems you have in trusting other people.

If you feel let down by your therapist in some ways, after having a good spell of therapy, it's best to discuss these feelings with the therapist in sessions before wanting to drop out, as it may be a form of "resistance". Therapy settings create an environment where your past difficulties with significant people in your life get re-enacted and worked on. It may be that your attitude to your therapist is a projection of your general attitude towards your parents or significant people in your life in the past. Even for those who are not in therapy, it might be helpful to examine their attitude to their parents as it can become a prototype of their relatedness to people in general as they grow up. Insights into these relationship difficulties in therapy settings can be very helpful and can help you work out different patterns with people you are close to in your current life.

A good, if rather lengthy, account of how early attachments operate and continue to influence people in later life is given by John Bowlby in his three volumes entitled *Separation*, *Loss* and *Attachment*.

So far we have talked about gaining insight into insecure attachments, which may offer insights about current dysfunctional patterns of relationships. However, people may be suffering because of difficulties with relationships they have with themselves and this often comes out in the form of symptoms like anxiety, depression or compulsive patterns of behaviour. In addition, it is important to realise that insight alone will not be curative and you will need to try out new ways of relating to yourself and other people and new ways of tackling problems in the real world.

The following points explain the mechanisms that underlie psychotherapeutic change process:

Getting connected with the inner distress

It is a normal tendency to avoid discomfort and seek pleasure; unfortunately, both these attitudes can affect our ability to deal with stress adversely. There are inner natural healing mechanisms that operate all the time. These mechanisms get accelerated when we come in contact with stress, very much like the release of pain-relieving chemicals (endorphins) when we experience bodily pain. A similar mechanism operates for the mind as well. Becoming aware of the inner distress activates certain homeostatic mechanisms that undo stress. The secret here is to allow yourself to experience distress without reacting emotionally to it or using your familiar patterns, such as avoidance activity or being dependent on substances or unhealthy relationships.

Reprocessing of old emotionally charged experiences

Psychotherapy offers an opportunity to revisit some of the unresolved issues from the past and understand them differently. Clients learn to reactivate these past experiences and relive them. Whilst reliving they try to understand these experiences differently thereby neutralising their emotional charge. As a result, clients are potentially freed from the restricting influences of these past experiences, because they have the opportunity to choose new ways of reacting to them.

Moving closer to reality

Psychotherapy enables us to look through our own defensive mechanisms (ways of distorting reality so that it becomes more acceptable to us). Defence mechanisms play an important role in coping with our daily stresses, but they need to be worked on if they result in psychological symptoms or impair our psychological functioning.

Changing attitudes and behaviours

Insight alone is not going to be sufficient if you're looking for solutions to real life problems, although it may produce improvements in your symptoms and how you feel about yourself. To improve your situation in the world you will need to have the courage to face up to aspects of your behaviour that need to change. Cognitive behavioural therapy is particularly good at helping you examine new strategies for coping with problems such as loneliness, phobias, addictions, anxieties, depressive thoughts, obsessions and compulsions, etc. For some people this means acquiring skills that they never had before and there is evidence that modelling behaviours using skilled role models, such as friends or therapists, may be the best way to acquire the skills. For others it is more a question of letting go of old patterns, so that they can put into place skills that already exist but are not being utilised.

If you feel you have to acquire completely new skills you may be well advised to choose a psychotherapy that offers access to some behavioural modelling and remember that it may take you a bit longer to acquire new skills.

Interpersonal skills, such as learning how to listen to others and empathise with them, are perhaps some of the most advanced human skills and take the longest to acquire.

Letting go of unrealistic goals and desires

Stress results when there is a big gap between our perception of where we are and where we should be. This gap can become bigger either because of a very low perception of self or very high inner standards of achievement. Psychotherapy can offer the opportunity to individuals to evaluate their abilities and readjust life goals to a more realistic level.

The important thing in psychotherapy is for you to undergo an experience that includes developing a trusting relationship, tackling the feared problems and trying out new ways of coping with them. It is probably wise to ensure that your therapist has adequate training and supervision and practises under a recognised code of ethics, which includes a complaints procedure should things go wrong.

The Essential Ingredients of Therapy

- A safe, warm, trusting relationship with a therapist who you feel understands you.
- Undoing avoidance: This means tackling emotionally painful experiences that you remain preoccupied with and that are currently causing you distress. This requires courage and determination. It is not necessary to bring up every unhappy topic in your past life. Things you have successfully forgotten or come to terms with can be left alone. It may be that some of your painful past experiences are not related to your current difficulties. They need not be discussed in therapy if you are not comfortable. The seeds of a bitter lemon may be left unexpressed.
- Understanding things differently: Understanding what lies behind your symptoms. Insight may not be essential, but it is often helpful.
- Trying out new ways of coping: Until you try out new forms of behaviour you cannot predict whether they make you feel better or worse. It takes courage to change and you will probably need to evaluate with your therapist whether the change is going in the right direction for you. Ultimately you are the best person to decide this for yourself.

Types of therapies commonly practised:

- Cognitive behavioural therapy: e.g. Beck's cognitive therapy for depression or rational emotive behavioural therapy (REBT).
- Psychoanalysis/psychodynamic: e.g. Freudian or Jungian psychoanalysis.
- Interpersonal therapy: e.g. Klerman and Weissman's interpersonal therapy for depression.

- Supportive psychotherapy: e.g. counselling using a humanistic approach, also called Rogerian or client-centred counselling.
- Integrative therapy: e.g. Cognitive Analytic Therapy (CAT).
- Existential therapy: e.g. Yalom's group therapy, logotherapy, daseinsanalysis.
- Other therapies that have research-based evidence of effectiveness include Gestalt therapy, art therapy, music therapy, psychodrama, neurolinguistic programming (NLP), systemic and family therapy, couples therapy, and pure behaviour therapy.

Most forms of psychotherapy can be carried out either in individual or group settings. People may be seen weekly, fortnightly, monthly or even less frequently. Most of the improvement from psychotherapy takes place in the first few sessions and if you have not benefitted from psychotherapy after about twenty sessions or one year's duration in therapy you probably aren't likely to do so. This word of caution may help you avoid the trap of becoming stuck in a long-term form of therapy, which is expensive and which is not producing change.

Different types of relaxation

There are a number of different ways in which one can relax. Historically music, dance, art, exercise, sport, reading and body massage, etc. have been used. Within the field of alternative medicine a number of different therapies have been tried, such as mindfulness meditation, Zen, yoga, tai chi, reflexology, Q gong, shiatsu, reiki, etc., with variable results.

Humanity has survived for nearly ten thousand years and mental health as a scientific discipline has existed only in the last hundred or so years. Our forefathers must have tried to find solutions to their stress and other psychological problems. They apparently did not have the benefit of the achievements of modern medicine, but there is no reason to believe that they were intellectually inferior to us and did not achieve anything meaningful. I, therefore, find it difficult to completely disregard and dismiss their attempts to discover something worthwhile that could have worked for them. It does not appear that modern psychiatry has done enough to scrutinise these ancient traditions. It seems that the time is now ripe to examine these various approaches with an open mind.

Within the field of science there are about a dozen different methods of relaxation that have been tried. The following list summarises some of these methods:

- Progressive muscle relaxation: Muscle tension is used here as a yardstick to measure stress. The individual learns to reduce mental stress by learning to relax muscles. This method is more likely to work if stress manifests in the form of muscle tension, headaches, chronic pain, etc.
- Guided imagery and visualisation: This involves creating positive images and fantasies that are antagonistic to the stress response.
- Breath regulation.
- Eye movement desensitisation.
- Stretching and physical exercise.
- Benson's concentration method.
- Self-awareness.
- Autogenic training.
- Alexander technique.
- Biofeedback treatment.
- Vipassana meditation.
- Mindfulness meditation.

The importance of breathing: Breath can be described as the royal road to one's bodily functions that are normally outside our control. Of all the body functions that are involved in producing stress response, breathing is the only function that is under our control and it happens autonomously at the same time. Scientific studies have proved that there are links between our lungs, heart, guts and brain. Any voluntary change in breathing results in changes in the functions of other organs as well. Breathing slowly (at the rate of six breaths per min), deeply and through the abdomen has a stabilising effect on the heart and gut motility.

Different schools of thought recommend different types of breathing as listed below:

- **Awareness of breathing (Anapana):** Awareness of one's own natural breath is an important first step in the practice of Vipassana meditation. Unlike the breath regulation techniques, such as abdominal breathing, it does not involve any conscious effort to change the pattern of one's normal breathing. The individual simply observes the natural flow of one's respiration and treats their thoughts and emotions as the background noise. This form of breath awareness brings about therapeutic change by way of:

- Shifts in the attention from negative emotional experiences to a neutral activity, such as breathing.
- Promoting present orientation – as clients focus intensely on an activity happening in the present moment.
- Stepping outside one's own thoughts and feelings as the act of observation of breath does not involve any thoughts and emotions.
- Improved mental concentration that helps in perception of inner bodily sensations.
- Changes in the level of consciousness.

Clients can practise this with the help of online instructions from meditation teacher Reverend Shri S. N. Goenka by way of accessing the website www.dhamma.org/en/about/mini_anapana

- **Abdominal breathing:** The practice of abdominal breathing has its roots in yoga and opera music traditions. Instead of expanding their chest during inspiration, clients learn to push the diaphragm down creating extra space in their chest to breathe in. Abdominal breathing has been found to help those who suffer from anxiety, panic attacks, hypertension, irritable bowel syndrome, premenstrual syndromes, etc.
- **Pelvic breathing:** Pelvic breathing is an extension of abdominal breathing wherein one practises abdominal breathing in a curled-up/ foetal position. It leads to relaxation of the whole pelvic floor and has therapeutic benefits in treatment of chronic pelvic pain, vaginismus, vulvodynia, etc.
- **Paced breathing:** Paced breathing is about prolonging the expiration, which leads to improved heart functions and it has been found useful in hypertension, postmenopausal hot flushes, anxiety and panic disorders.

Unhealthy patterns of breathing:

• Hyperventilation	• Reverse breathing
• Throat holding	• Clavicular breathing
• Breath holding	• Sighing

Different Types of Therapy

Existential therapy

Existentialism is a branch of philosophy that deals with felt emotions and certain core issues of human life, such as death anxiety, search for meaning in life, anxiety related to making the right choice, taking responsibility for one's emotions and actions, etc. Existentialism encourages clients to confront their inner pain rather than find an escape into the distractions of everyday life.

Existentialism, therefore, is not just about reducing our stress levels but increasing our capacity to tolerate stress.

The main aim of the existential therapy is to enrich our lives by living more fully and enhancing awareness of both the positive and the negative. Symptom cure is seen as a by-product of therapy. It can also be achieved by restricting our habitual way of living, but that would limit the joys of life as well.

Characteristics of existential psychotherapy

- It deals with the core issues of human life.
- Inevitability of stress; one cannot not experience stress. No matter what decision we make every decision is followed by some stress.
- It does not seek to eliminate all the negative forces within oneself. It helps clients make sense of the negative forces and come to terms with something that is basic to human life.
- Ontic v ontological suffering: ontic suffering is remediable whereas ontological is not. One-third of human suffering can be described as inevitable and the remaining two-thirds is there because we are trying to get that one-third out of our system.
- Psychiatric problems are understood as the individual's failure to come to terms with one's existential reality, which in many ways is common

to all humanity, i.e. struggle to find ultimate meaning in life, coping with the unpredictable nature of human life and the possibility of death, feeling isolated and alone, conflict over choice (am I doing the right thing?), responsibility and free will.

- Death anxiety is natural, but we seek to avoid it by not thinking and talking about it. Anxiety about death is what underlies many of the clinical symptoms. It is a taboo subject and people are discouraged from talking about it. Not avoiding the topic of death can lead to what is described as "death desensitisation", which is considered desirable in existential therapy.

- We limit our capacity to experience joy and inner peace by always trying to escape from this "burdensome character of Being" into the distractions of everyday life. Heidegger (1927) describes our most common everyday mood as "the pallid, evenly balanced lack of mood", which contains traces of irritation and boredom. Everyday activity is often an escape from that mood – we refuse to look at "the burdensome character of Being". Existentialism encourages us to confront it.

- Non-directive; therapists do not see themselves as experts who have answers to all the problems that clients bring in the session. They don't have a map for patients to move from point A to B, as they allow the patients to decide which direction they want to go in. They are willing to work along with clients to make sense of their experiences and help them move on from the place they are stuck in emotionally.

Therapy Process

Death desensitisation

There is a general reluctance among mental health professionals and clients to dwell on this subject in clinical settings even though many of the psychological symptoms stem from one's insecurities about one's non-existence. It is assumed that a discussion on this topic will make our clients feel worse, following Adolph Meyer's adage, "Don't scratch where it doesn't itch."

In fact, the thoughts of our own and that of our loved one's mortality are itching us all the time. We may not realise it as it can manifest itself in a variety of disguises: panic attacks, nostalgic feelings, insecure attachments and separation anxiety, fear of travelling, crowded places and flights are some such examples. I have found in my clinical practice that allowing ourselves to think about death can enhance our own enjoyment of life. Thinking about death will not bring it sooner, but it can make our lives look much brighter in contrast.

I would like to narrate a little incident that happened with a friend of mine several years ago. He saw a mole on his skin getting bigger and bigger and wondered if it was some kind of cancerous growth. He went to his doctor who took his concern seriously and sent him for a biopsy. My friend waited eagerly for the results and on the day he had to go to see the doctor for the result he was in a real state of panic. He couldn't sleep the previous night and had shakes in the morning. He could hardly eat his breakfast. He was much relieved when the doctor told him that it was all clear and there was no malignancy.

My friend came home and took a day off from work. He spent the day with his wife and children, went to see a movie and ate at a fancy restaurant. Later that week he described that day as the best day of his life. Apparently he did not eat anything that he had not eaten before and the movie he saw was not an out of this world movie. What made that day the best day of his life? It was the awareness of death and the fact that he was still alive.

A constant awareness of death can make us celebrate our lives. A confrontation with death can create a dramatic perspective-altering opportunity. Yalom (2002) has discussed the experiences of cancer patients and the wisdom that comes in the face of death, quoting his patients' lament "what a pity I had to wait for wisdom until now, till my body was riddled with cancer".

Existentialism reminds us that death is not something that will happen to us some day in the remote future, but something that is happening every minute of our lives. Those of us who cannot come to terms with this realisation end up having clinical anxiety, which is just a camouflage for death anxiety with many individuals. A constant awareness of death gives life its significance.

Existential issues to ponder upon

- Every relationship has its boundaries and beyond those boundaries we are on our own. I was born alone and I will go from this world alone; no one will go with me. I accept this as an essential human condition and see every togetherness that I experience in this world as a boon.

- No one has ever been able to understand me 100% and no one ever will. The gap is unbridgeable, but that doesn't mean we cannot enjoy togetherness in our lives.
- What a strange thing that this world is full of millions of people, but still people feel lonely. Seeing the potential friends among strangers can be helpful.

Biofeedback Therapy

Biofeedback has been defined as a group of therapeutic procedures that utilise external devices (mechanical, electronic or computer) to measure and feed back to the individual information about their stress levels and other physiological functions. These devices can act as a mirror to the mind and the feedback can help individuals achieve a greater awareness and control over their stress.

The external devices may not be required if one is able to establish connections with one's inner state of affairs, as it happens in certain types of meditations.

With the help of biofeedback devices it has been possible to change even the functions that are normally outside our control, such as heart rate, peripheral blood flow, skin temperature, brain wave pattern and smooth muscle activity.

Unfortunately, until recently, the use of biofeedback treatment was limited in medicine and more so in psychiatry. Its lack of popularity in the past could be related to not having very sophisticated equipment that could measure the subtle changes in our body functions and convert them into tangible signals. It is only in recent years that the popularity of this treatment method has grown.

The research done in the last decade or so has consistently shown physiological changes in the EEG pattern, heart rate variability, respiratory rhythm, etc. not just in anxiety disorders but in other psychiatric illnesses as well and has opened a new door for psychiatric patients. There now appears to be a distinct role for applied psychophysiology and biofeedback therapy in the management of psychiatric disorders.

Historical background

Biofeedback therapy was first discovered in the late 1950s in the United States of America following the realisation that one can change the physiology of one's body by changing the mind. It has its roots in many disciplines, such as behaviour therapy, cybernetics, psychophysiology and EEG, consciousness and stress management.

Claude Bernard, a physician, developed the concept of physiological homeostasis, which became integral to the discipline of physiology. Illnesses were thought to occur because some homeostatic feedback mechanism was malfunctioning and a similar homeostatic imbalance was thought to explain stress (Schwartz and Olson, 2003). The pioneering work done by Cannon (1929) and Selye (1956) led to the understanding that the physiological stress response and psychosomatic illnesses were results of breakdown in the homeostatic mechanisms. This understanding paved the way for the use of biofeedback therapy in stress disorders.

Psycho-cybernetics

Cybernetics is the principle that can explain the self-regulatory function of systems, both animate and inanimate. It is based on the assumption of circular causality (i.e. that the output of a system can be used as an input for the same system in order to modify its function). This principle works for control of temperature in the room with the help of a thermostat. In living organisms, described as homeostasis, it helps in maintaining the blood pressure and blood sugar with the help of baro-receptors and chemo-receptors respectively.

The pain control within the body can also be explained on the same principle, i.e. the sensation of pain acts as a feedback signal to the brain, which leads to release of endorphins (body's natural pain killers) resulting in reduction of pain sensation.

The same principle applies to the mind as well and this science has been described as psycho-cybernetics. It is about providing feedback to the mind on the physiology or behaviour of an individual, which can lead to regulation or control of the abnormal experience, function or behaviour.

These homeostatic mechanisms work best only if the individual chooses to stay connected with the inner feedback signals. From a psychiatric point of view, this would mean staying connected with the inner distress and not reacting emotionally.

Biofeedback therapy and meditative practices help the clients get in touch with their inner stress without reacting emotionally to it (or learning to stay relaxed at the same time) hence promoting these homeostatic mechanisms.

The role of cybernetic principles in biofeedback therapy has been explained in terms of a number of different models, i.e. operant conditioning, homeostasis, information processing (Anliker, 1977), etc. From a cybernetic perspective, operant conditioning is one form of feedback. The individual performs some mental tasks that result in reduction (or increase) in stress scores and this feedback in the form of positive (or negative) results of a particular behaviour acts as a reinforcer.

How does biofeedback work?

At a very simple level, biofeedback seems to work in the same way a mirror works for improving one's physical appearance. Biofeedback has been described as a mirror to the mind or a camera on the unconscious. A simple awareness of something that the person was not conscious of can be therapeutic as in some instances the individual has already got the ability to take remedial measures. For example, a client became aware, during a muscle tension (EMG) feedback session, that the tension in his shoulder muscles was 50 microvolts, as compared to the normal value of 5 microvolts, and was able to reduce it by adopting simple relaxation methods.

Indications for use of biofeedback therapy

The biofeedback therapy has been successfully used in the following disorders:

- Anxiety and panic disorders
- Depressive disorders
- Alcohol and drug misuse disorders
- Epilepsy
- Attention deficit and hyperactivity disorders

- Psychosomatic disorders, such as tension headaches and migraines, irritable bowel syndrome, asthma and hypertension
- Other disorders: urinary and faecal incontinence, vulvodynia, Raynaud's disease

Contraindications of biofeedback therapy

- Acute agitation where the client is unlikely to participate in the treatment process
- Severe depression with suicidal ideation
- Manic disorder
- Paranoid states
- Severe OCD
- Acute medical decompensation
- Potential for dissociation, depersonalisation and fugue states

Parameters of stress that can be measured

- Increased muscle tension
- Increased respiratory rate
- Lowered skin temperature
- Increased heart rate (seen during panic attacks)
- EEG changes in the alpha, theta, delta, beta waves
- Galvanic skin resistance
- Peripheral blood flow indicative of vasoconstriction seen in anxiety disorders

Important Concepts

Heart rate variability

The rate at which the heart beats varies from beat to beat even in healthy and normal states. In fact, it is considered desirable to have a greater variation in heart beat as it has been reported that heart rate variability is low in disease states. A measure of variability, usually the standard deviation of the R wave to R wave inter-beat interval on ECG, is indicative of autonomic control of the heart and perhaps also the lungs, the gut and certain facial muscles (Gevirtz and Lehrer, 2003).

This variability, called heart rate variability (HRV), is controlled by two pathways within the autonomic nervous system: the sympathetic and parasympathetic. A decreased HRV is associated with increased cardiac mortality and morbidity. Research has discovered a link between respiration rhythm and heart rhythm. A rhythmic braking and speeding of the heart rate is associated with respiration. With inhalation, the vagal (parasympathetic) braking on heart rate is removed and thus heart rate is speeded up. The opposite happens during expiration, the vagal brake is reapplied and it slows the rate down again. This heart rate/respiration rhythm is called respiratory sinus arrhythmia (RSA).

The finding that heart rate changes with respiration has allowed researchers to modify heart rate by way of altering respiratory rhythm. The most commonly used respiratory pattern in biofeedback treatment is abdominal breathing.

The role of breathing in biofeedback therapy

Breath can be described as the royal road to one's physiology that is normally outside one's control. Breathing is one of the very few functions that are voluntary and at the same time autonomous.

Breathing slowly (at the rate of five to seven breaths per minute), deeply and into the abdomen (leading to flattening of diaphragm) has been reported to have a stabilising effect on the heart and gut motility, thereby making one's body immune to the effects of stress.

Different schools of thought recommend different types of breathing as listed below:

Abdominal breathing: The practice of abdominal breathing has its roots in yoga and music (opera) traditions. Instead of expanding their upper chest during inhalation, clients learn to push the diaphragm down creating extra space in their chest to breathe in. The individual can see their abdomen rise and fall during respiration while the upper chest remains relatively still. Abdominal breathing has been found to help those who suffer from anxiety, panic attacks, hypertension, irritable bowel syndrome, premenstrual syndromes, sinus tachycardia, etc.

Awareness of breathing (anapana): Awareness of one's own natural breath is an important first step in the practice of Vipassana meditation (www.dhamma.org). Unlike the breath regulation techniques such as abdominal breathing, it does not involve any conscious effort to change the pattern of one's normal breathing.

The individual simply observes the natural flow of one's respiration and treats one's thoughts and emotions as the background noise. This form of breathing can be seen as a form of biofeedback where the individual becomes aware of the abnormal patterns of breathing, such as hyperventilation, breath holding, sighing, etc. A simple awareness of the abnormal pattern can result in resumption of the normal pattern.

The rationale for using biofeedback therapy in psychiatric disorders

Physiological abnormalities have been reported in a number of psychiatric disorders, such as anxiety disorders, depressive disorders, alcohol and substance misuse, attention deficit and hyperactivity disorders, and epilepsy.

Anxiety disorders

The activation of sweat glands as part of sympathetic over-activity in anxiety disorders has been known to mental health professionals for some time, but the devices available at the time were not very accurate or user friendly. The other features of sympathetic over-activity seen in anxiety patients are peripheral vasoconstriction, hyperventilation, increased muscle tone, reduced heart rate variability, etc.

The research on heart rate variability has helped reformulate biological theories of anxiety, shifting the focus away from sympathetic nervous system disturbances in favour of a study of the balance between sympathetic and parasympathetic nervous system activity, which is disturbed in anxiety disorders.

A reduced heart rate variability has been found in several anxiety disorder patients who are found to be at increased risk for coronary heart disease, including sudden death. Individuals with high levels of anxiety have a 4.5 to 6.0 fold increase in risk for sudden cardiac death compared to individuals with no anxiety (Grillon, 2005).

Depressive disorders

Patients suffering from depression have been found to have a right-left asymmetry in the alpha brain wave activity on EEG and this finding has been reported in the offspring of patients suffering from depression who have not had depressive illness.

The right frontal lobe is supposed to be involved in the organisation and production of negative emotions and avoidance behaviour. Any damage or deactivation of this part of the brain can result in hypomanic symptoms.

The opposite is true for depression, i.e. left frontal lobe is involved in organisation and production of positive emotions and approach behaviour, and brain insult in this area can cause symptoms of depression (Davidson, 1995).

Deactivation of certain brain areas has been reported to be associated with high alpha activity in that area, which can be modified with the help of neurofeedback therapy.

Neurofeedback therapy

Neurofeedback has been used successfully in attention deficit and hyperactivity disorders (ADHD), epilepsy, anxiety disorders, mood disorders, traumatic brain injury, and alcohol and substance misuse.

There is some evidence to indicate that ADHD patients have reduced beta-wave activity in their brains. Beta waves are commonly associated with cortical arousal. These children, who have under-aroused brains, indulge in hyperactive behaviour in order to bring their cortical arousal to an optimal level. With neurofeedback training these children can be trained to enhance beta activity, which has therapeutic value.

It has been demonstrated that anxiety disorder patients have fewer alpha waves and more beta waves. This pattern can be altered with the help of EEG feedback.

The biofeedback protocols for anxiety disorders include alpha and theta enhancement. Combined alpha-theta EEG feedback procedures have also been successfully used in treating patients with addictive behaviour such as alcoholism (Ochs, 1992; Peniston and Kulkosky, 1990).

A Holistic Way to Relax

This can be described as "a new way to chill out". The objective of this exercise is to give rest to your mind for at least a few hours so that it can heal itself and neutralise the stress that your mind accumulates on a daily basis.

This exercise is best done twice a day (i.e. half an hour in the morning soon after getting up and for about an hour in the evening). You could have a longer session on Sunday evenings if possible, when you have finished all the weekend jobs and there is no more work to be done that day apart from the necessary daily activities, such as eating meals and getting ready for bed.

You can start with just one or two ideas that you like from the list below and think around them for as long as you feel like. It would be desirable to gradually build up the time incorporating more of these ideas.

It would be a wonderful thing if we had the ability to switch our thoughts (mind) on and off the way we switch our car engine off, but it's not in our control to switch off the mind's engine – our mind never rests, it is active even in deep sleep. We cannot rest our minds the way we rest our bodies (i.e. stop working and put our feet up). We may not be able to switch off the engine of our minds, but we can certainly put it in a neutral gear and that's when it starts healing itself more than when we are sleeping.

This exercise will take you through certain steps that are the opposite of what happens inside your mind when stress is produced.

There is no need to stop physical activity completely, although there are some restrictions on certain activities as mentioned in the following paragraphs. There is no need to try and empty your mind as it would be almost impossible for you to do so when you start off on this journey. The mind needs an object to focus on all the time. If we stop giving our mind new experiences, it starts dwelling on the past ones – resulting in inner unfolding.

The most important aspect of this exercise is not to react emotionally, both positively and negatively and, if that is not possible at a given point in time, to see through one's emotional reactivity without getting upset.

This exercise might help you get connected with your inner stress and there may be occasions when instead of feeling relaxed you might feel more stressed. If you do feel that your stress level is going up during this session it only means that you are moving closer to your goal of working on your stress. Do not carry on with the session if you find the stress intolerable. In that case it should be done in the presence of your therapist who is willing to guide you through the session.

When doing a longer session please make a checklist of pending jobs that you have put off until the next day so that they won't bother you during this session.

During this time you are choosing to be on your own and have informed your family members not to disturb you. You have no mental checklist of doing things during this time, but would be open to doing anything that comes up at the spur of the moment.

Activities that are prohibited: drinking alcohol or smoking, watching television, listening to radio/music, reading newspapers/magazines/books, talking to a friend over the phone or anything that can create both positive and/or negative emotions.

Permitted activities: breathing exercises or other forms of relaxation (without music), walking (without being curious about the outside world), washing dishes, gardening, cleaning, routine domestic activities that will not lead to emotional ups and downs, mild stretching exercises, lying or sitting for relaxation.

Imagine that your mind is like a mansion, a part of it is fully cluttered and disorganised – it is the part of the mind that is full of negative emotions, such as anxiety, worry, depression, fear, anger, hatred, etc.

Another part of this mansion is very clean, ornate and beautiful, full of fragrance, beautiful paintings, decorations, expensive linen and furniture, delicious food and you are with your loved ones in there; that is the happy side of your mind.

And then a part of this mansion is neither good nor bad. It has got nothing that is extraordinary, cheerful or distressing, and you are choosing to stay in this area during the period of this exercise. You are neither trying to tidy the cluttered parts nor are you trying to enjoy the comforts and happiness of the second part of the mansion, instead you are choosing to quietly move into the part of the mansion that is devoid of the happiness and sadness of everyday life. It represents the inner peace and tranquillity and is beyond the reach of the worldly emotions of happiness and sadness.

Find a quiet corner of the room, dim the lights, switch off mobile phones, wear loose clothes and feel free to keep changing posture as you please.

Now start the exercise by saying the following to yourself:

- I have done all the pending work that needed doing; there is no more work to be done in the next hour or so. This time is mine to relax and get connected with my deeper self.
- I accept the way I am. I accept fully my race, the colour of my hair and skin, my height and weight, all the imperfections of my appearance, my age, my parents, my siblings, my spouse, my children. I accept my mind and all its mood swings; I accept all my assets and imperfections.
- I am choosing to give rest to my mind and my mind can rest to its maximum when it is not making any judgements about people, things and situations. At least for the duration of this exercise, I am choosing not to make any judgements such as good/bad, right/wrong, ugly/beautiful, rich/poor, intelligent/stupid, kind/cruel, nice/nasty about anything, etc. What seems to be a good thing now might turn out to be a bad one in the long run, and vice versa.
- I can understand my past in terms of historical inevitability – things that have happened so far in my life had to happen that way; they couldn't have happened any other way. That was my destiny. I couldn't have changed things even if I wanted to. I therefore choose not to think about my past during this exercise.
- I look upon all my past failures as my teacher; they have important lessons for me. I may not have got what I wanted in life, but in the process I have learned important lessons of life. These experiences have made me wiser and my life richer.
- I am choosing not to dwell on my future, my life goals, my desires, my dreams, etc. Not thinking about my future plans for a while is not going to cause irreparable loss to me. I will be okay even if my life goals are not met; there will still be possibilities of happiness.
- I let go of all my desires for at least the next few hours and it might enable me to experience inner peace and tranquillity. I am therefore choosing to live in the present moment, whatever it has to offer without wanting anything different. I am okay with this feeling that nothing much is happening in my life at the moment.

- I do not expect anything from this world and I do not have any desire to give anything to anyone. Other people's possessions are like dust for me.

- I want to give rest to my desire to make this world a better place or to make a difference in this world by my actions.

- I decide to become action-orientated rather than result-orientated. I am not in full control of the results of my actions, as there are a lot of factors out there that I have no control over. These factors keep influencing the outcome of my actions. I let go of my preoccupation with the results and focus only on my actions. I have stopped waiting for the results of my actions. Things happen when the time is ripe and I do not set any time limits for getting the results. If the action is positive, the result has to be positive; I surrender the results to my destiny or higher forces if there are any.

- All things are impermanent; nothing stays forever. Every thought and every feeling dies its natural death, if I choose not to participate in it by making judgements about it and emotionally reacting to it. The thoughts and feelings that I am experiencing now are not going to stay in my mind forever. Sooner or later they will go, just like a guest who stays in a guest house. There is no need to get excited about having a nice thought and no need to get upset about having a bad thought. Just as the owner of the guest house doesn't get excited when a nice person comes to stay in his guest house and doesn't get upset if an unpleasant person stays there, as they know that their stay is temporary.

- The majority of the thoughts that enter my mind do not accurately represent the reality out there. They need to be fine-tuned in order for me to appreciate the reality, but I am not choosing to do that job now. For now, I am choosing not to make any judgements about them. I make peace with all the thoughts, both positive and negative, that are there in my mind – I neither try to suppress them nor try to act on them.

- I choose not to compare myself with others, as each individual is unique in many ways. Each one of us has our own failures and successes, which happen at different points in time. Comparisons can create a false sense of inferiority or superiority if we are not careful.

Right now I want to be myself and celebrate my life. I do not wish to be somebody else.

- I am trying not to wish ill on anybody. I have no intention of causing hurt or harm to anyone. If someone has caused problems to me in the past I see it as my destiny and let nature decide the consequences of their actions. Wanting to see justice done at once is an unnecessary burden that I am carrying on my shoulders.
- I want to use this time to think about all those people I might have hurt willingly or unwillingly in the past. In my mind I say sorry to them and resolve not to say or do things with the intention of causing hurt to anyone.
- I think of all those who might have hurt me willingly or unwillingly in the past and I understand this in terms of their imperfections and being human. I pardon them. I am trying to let go of even the justified anger, resentment and bitterness as they hurt me as much as the unjustified ones. By forgiving people I am certainly doing myself a big favour.
- I am for the time being putting aside my desire to be somebody and reach somewhere. I have no desire to leave my footprints in the history of events.

I am grateful to Mark Pearson, a consultant psychotherapist and my psychotherapy supervisor who very kindly reviewed this chapter and gave helpful suggestions.

CHAPTER 8

Coping with Stress

How do people cope normally? What is normal coping? And what is abnormal? Am I suffering from stress that needs management? Is it possible that normal individuals also use unhealthy coping mechanisms or need stress management? Can a normal person who doesn't suffer from any clinical symptoms also benefit from psychological approaches? How to know whether my coping style is healthy or unhealthy?

These questions come to mind quite normally, but generally people don't go to great lengths in trying to find answers to them. It seems appropriate to think deeply about these issues if one is looking for ways of improving one's well-being.

Psychoanalysis teaches us how to find meaning in our thoughts and feelings, and cognitive therapists help us find alternate and more rational thoughts that can replace our existing illogical thoughts. The experiential therapists, on the other hand, emphasise the need to undo our negative feelings without bothering about the thoughts.

Gautama the Buddha, on the other hand, suggested a totally different and unique solution to the problems, which is becoming very popular worldwide in modern times and the scientific community seems to have embraced it.

His approach discourages us from fighting with our thoughts and feelings, and explains how we can detach ourselves from them with the objective of managing them better. Every thought and every feeling dies its natural death if we don't make a judgement about it, join in with it, react to it, resist it, identify with it, etc. Instead if we can simply observe it with our emotionally neutral consciousness it loses its hold on us and we can manage it better. No matter how horrible or exciting a thought is, we don't question its coming to our mind and choose not to react to it emotionally during the time of reflection, and this helps us deal with it better.

An understanding of the normal healing mechanisms and how stress is produced is essential here before we can discuss coping mechanisms and specific strategies of coping with stress.

The following basic assumptions can help us understand stress and coping with it.

- The human body is largely self-renewing and so is the mind. Nature has given us all the ability to undo stress. There are no new lessons to be learned in managing stress; all we need is to unlearn the lessons of stress that we have learned so far. It is easy to understand that we all get stressed in difficult situations and we would reach a breaking point if we did not have the ability to neutralise this stress. The fact that we don't reach a breaking point proves that there must be inner healing mechanisms.

- This natural ability to undo stress operates through a homeostatic mechanism that works in our minds and is driven by biological processes that result in lowering of stress levels. These homeostatic mechanisms come into force only when we come into contact with our inner stress. These mechanisms are switched off if we cut ourselves off from the inner stress signals. The mechanism is similar to that of a thermostat – higher room temperature leads to switching off of the heating system and a lower temperature switches it on. Health professionals are aware that a similar mechanism governs our blood pressure, blood sugar, hormonal secretions and many other functions in the body.

- The mind heals itself best when it is not constantly receiving new experiences through the five senses. It may be that when we feel that nothing much is happening in our lives, deep in our minds healing is taking place. It is therefore important to seek periods of solitude for this daily repair to take place.

- Stress is made up of our mental reactions, with their accompanying physiological changes, to a given situation. This mental reaction happens as a result of our judgements about people, things and situations. The stress response can be modified by changing the way we make judgements about things, people and situations.

- Even positive experiences can generate stress. Seeking excitement that our minds are not used to can lead to stress. Seeing life as one big party and trying to get the maximum out of it can be counter-productive. Constant focus on achieving goals can lead to increased levels of stress. Being always on the go and doing something positive does not allow our minds to rest, heal and grow psychologically.

- Distraction on to something "positive" is not a good solution to the problem. It is good to be able to switch off and turn our attention to something positive as it helps us distance ourselves from the negative, but it does not make the negative disappear. The negative then gets buried in our unconscious mind. It has to be dealt with on its own terms.

- Living in the present moment reduces stress, whereas preoccupation with the past and the future can lead to increased levels of stress. If we think deeply, we mostly get stressed when we think about what has just happened or what is going to happen soon. If we have the ability to switch off thoughts of the past and the future we can cut out a lot of stress for ourselves. One might argue that planning for the future and learning from the mistakes of the past are important, but these should not require more than just 5% of our time and can also be seen as present tasks. What is undesirable is brooding over the past and future.

- There are two types of happiness: inner and outer. The happiness of the external world is about achieving something that is important to you. This happiness is dependent upon external conditions and it disappears when the conditions change. The second kind of happiness can be described as inner peace or tranquillity, which is not dependent on the external conditions. It can happen as a result of letting go of one's obsession with worldly happiness.

The coping mechanisms that we normally use are:

- Taking a break from one's normal routine by going on holiday.
- Distracting oneself on to something else, e.g. watching television, going to a party, seeking friends, etc. This works on the same principle of suspending the activity that was causing the stress in the first place.
- Drinking or taking drugs, which leads to alterations in consciousness and obliteration of the feelings and sensation of stress.
- **Suppression:** adopting a stiff upper lip attitude. The individual makes a conscious attempt to modify one's actions or expression of one's emotions. The emotions remain under control, but don't disappear.
- **Repression**: thoughts and emotions are suppressed into the unconscious mind, but this happens without the awareness of the individual and is outside the control of the individual.
- **Denial:** truth is denied when the individual finds themselves unable to accept it. There are different types of denial – normal, neurotic, psychotic, etc.
- **Projection:** what is denied in oneself is then projected onto others with the objective of face-saving or denial of responsibility and the guilt that comes with it. Blaming others for one's own faults is a common example, and it takes the form of being suspicious and paranoid in clinical conditions. The hostile feeling inside oneself get projected on to others who then become the feared object.
- **Displacement:** a common example is when a boss takes out his anger on his assistant, who in turn takes it out on their spouse, who in turn takes it out on the child, and who then kicks the dog. Emotions is displaced from its original context, which is very complicated, to an innocuous situation that is easy to work on and less embarrassing. Fear of one's father takes on the shape of fear of crowded places or horses, which is less embarrassing and easy to express in front of others.
- **Anticipation:** being mindful of any possible stress event in the future enables us to manage it in small chunks and get desensitised to it before it actually happens. This capacity to perceive future danger

and emotions helps in mastering it in small steps. Scientific research indicates that a moderate amount of anxiety before surgery promotes post-surgical adaptation, and anticipatory mourning facilitates adaptation of parent of children suffering from terminal illnesses.

- **Humour**: encourages us not to take painful matters too seriously and protects us from the harmful effects of negative emotions.

A careful look at the above list suggests that a lot of coping is about our inability to accept the painful realities of our existence, which then results in our attempts to distort it.

Healthy Coping

Stress can be prevented or reduced by means of the following three approaches:

- Reducing the demands on us
- Changing our perception
- Increasing our coping abilities

Reducing the demand

- Individuals suffering from high levels of anxiety and stress feel overwhelmed by external demands and they can benefit from changing their lifestyle (i.e. slowing down, making fewer commitments and pulling back from certain tasks). Making changes in the immediate environment and reflecting on how one spends time and plans future activities could be important.

Change of perception

- Not judging people, situations and things unless one has to because of their role in society: we cannot expect to live normal lives without making judgements about ourselves and about others. Judgements are required when we are actively engaged with life. Unfortunately, we tend to overdo it and this has a tiring effect on our minds. During periods of rest and inner healing it would be helpful if we gave rest to our minds by suspending our judgement for short periods of time. Even at other times, it might be helpful if we reflected on our habit of making unnecessary judgements, judgements that we can do without. In most situations we do not know the inside stories of people's lives, hence our judgements can be subjective and biased.

- Letting go: does not mean losing control over things. On the contrary, it can mean allowing things to happen, things that were being blocked due to our resistance.
- Seeing opportunities in every situation can be helpful in managing negative emotions.
- Understanding every emotion and situation in terms of its impermanent nature.

Increasing our coping abilities

- Finding time to chill out every day: Creating time slots for relaxation exercises in everyday life is better than taking long holidays. I generally recommend clients to set aside at least half an hour in the morning and about an hour in the evening when they have planned nothing in particular. It might sound like wasting time, but I call it "wasting time creatively". How to do it is discussed in chapter 7 of this book.
- Writing a stress diary: A stress diary can provide useful information related to your stress profile and can be helpful in working on a stress management plan. Thinking about what you could have done in a given situation and rehearsing your responses if a similar situation arose in the future can increase your chances of acting differently next time it happens.

Other tips

- Going to bed, not when tired or sleepy, but when wide awake. This will allow time to practise some relaxation exercises before going to sleep and it is likely to improve the quality of your sleep.
- Preventing tiredness is better than relaxing after one has become tired. Taking short breaks several times during the day can be helpful. There

are three types of breaks – micro (for up to thirty seconds) breaks to be taken every ten to fifteen minutes; mini (five to ten minutes) breaks to be taken every hour; and mega (up to half an hour) every three to four hours.

- Having a few extra minutes before an activity to prepare the mind to deal with the task, and a few minutes after it, to let our mind process the stress resulting from the activity.
- Using the times when you feel bored or feel you are wasting time by practising relaxation, e.g. whilst waiting in a queue at a supermarket check-out or before an appointment.
- Visualisation and imagining yourself behaving in a calm and relaxed manner can be tried, but the chances of its success are greater if the visualisation involves not just the external behaviour but your identity (i.e. identity of a calm person in control, such as a parent, teacher and leader) as well.
- In Ancient Greek language there is a word – *eutrapelia* – to describe productive use of leisure. If you are serious about solving your problems, you should carefully choose what you do when you are not solving them. Possibly you like complicated puzzles, chess or other intellectual games. You may enjoy them, but they tire you. Practising silence creates space in your mind for creative ideas related to what you have been thinking. If one has been practising silence every day, one would notice that solutions to our everyday problems crop up during periods of silence. It may be because it's easier for a quiet mind to find solutions to our problems than a busy mind.
- Live as if you were already living for the second time and had acted for the first time as wrongly as you are going to act now.

Equanimity – A Well-Being Tool and the Goal

Do I have sufficient balance of mind to tackle my strong emotions?

Equanimity is the balance of mind or a state of emotional neutrality that is needed to deal with our strong emotions. It means being neither too excited nor too upset about anything in particular and being on an even keel.

Equanimity is not a sterile neutrality where there is a longing to experience strong emotions in order to escape life's perceived emptiness or nothingness. It does not mean a total lack of emotions. This state of neutrality is accompanied by a feeling of tranquillity and inner peace that replaces our day-to-day emotions, such as fears, anxieties, sadness and pleasure.

It is a normal human tendency to seek happiness all the time and we are constantly looking for positive emotions and thoughts. There is nothing wrong with this, but when it comes to undoing our inner stress (or negative emotions) it is essential that we are in an emotionally neutral state. We cannot neutralise a negative emotion simply by creating a positive one, as the positive emotion pushes the negative one aside or into the unconscious mind. These negative emotions can resurface at any time. The negative emotions have to be dealt with on their own terms.

In order to deal with the negative emotions we need to be in an emotionally neutral state (i.e. be equanimous).

Equanimity is required for emotional healing very much like needing clean water to wash dirty linen. Emotions can be understood in terms of different colours, which colour our consciousness. Just as we cannot use coloured water for washing our clothes, the mind that is already coloured emotionally, both with positive and negative emotions, cannot be used for inner healing. Stress can be visualised in terms of both positive and negative emotions. Even positive emotions cause stress (i.e. being excited about a project, going on a date, attending a party, inviting people over and winning the lottery – all these can cause stress).

We can handle these positive emotions better if a part of our mind is equanimous (i.e. not completely submerged in the emotion).

In order for our minds to undo stress we need to plan and set aside some time every day when we are neither seeking excitement or positive emotions nor putting ourselves in situations that can cause negative emotions. These periods should be when nothing much is happening and we let ourselves be in these moments. We normally don't like such moments, but these are exactly the moments when inner psychological stress is being undone.

Since childhood we are told not to waste time, be creative, focused and proactive. This puts pressure on us to be more successful, rich and famous and we fail to realise that we need to set some time aside from these pursuits of achievement to let go and undo the stress that accumulates every day.

Being equanimous does not mean that one stops enjoying all the positive emotions. It is possible that in the middle of experiencing a positive or a negative emotion a part of our mind is experiencing the emotion and the rest of it is observing it. This split is very important in trying to manage our emotions and affairs of everyday life.

If we are not totally submerged in an experience we can handle it better. Learning to be equanimous helps us to achieve that goal.

The next question is – how to be equanimous?

There are a number of mental tools that can be employed to achieve a state of equanimity. A few of them are mentioned here:

1. The principle of impermanence
2. Noticing more, judging less
3. Disowning mental experiences that don't belong to us
4. Writing an emotion diary
5. Attention regulation

Noticing more, judging and reacting less

> *I can't even cope with what I already know; what is the point in noticing more? Won't I get more stressed?*

The problem is not awareness or knowledge. It's how we react to it. In fact, noticing and reacting mentally compete with each other and if we focus more on noticing things it will make us react less.

If I knew everything about everybody

- *About their past and about their future*
- *About their joys and about their sorrows*
- *About their fears and about their hopes*
- *About their successes and about their failures*
- *About their relationships and about their loneliness*
- *About their illnesses and about their health*
- *About their abilities and about their disabilities*
- *About their riches and about their poverty*
- *About their cruelty and about their kindness*

- *About their confidence and about their insecurities*
- *And also knew all of those about myself*

I would:

- *Neither be angry with nor afraid of anybody*
- *Neither be in awe nor contemptuous of anybody*
- *Neither be intrusive nor indifferent to anybody*
- *Neither be greedy nor overly charitable to anybody*
- *Neither be afraid of nor dominant with anybody*
- *Neither be attracted to nor be repulsed by anybody*

I would always be:

- *Kind to myself and others*
- *Loving with myself and others*
- *Forgiving to myself and others*
- *Happy when I see someone happy*
- *Compassionate when I see someone unhappy*
- *Able to separate others' actions from them*
- *Inspired by their successes*

Nothing would:

- *Shock me or shake me out of my equanimity*
- *Break my friendly feelings towards them*

I would understand that we all are:

- *Made of the same bricks and mortar*
- *Hopelessly/hopefully similar to each other*
- *Similar in our fears, insecurities, desires and hopes*
- *On the same journey; some a bit ahead, others a bit behind*

I will truly become a free human being

Noticing more can be both an active as well as a passive process; active when we consciously make an effort to perceive/experience more, this can make us react less. On the other hand, it could be a passive process, an outcome of reacting less. If we choose to react less, more of our consciousness is available for observation, freed from reacting and can be engaged in noticing.

No judgements – no stress

The following chain reaction of information processing explains how stress is produced following any incident. Our judgements are the links between the external situation and our stress response. Suspension of our judgements will result in suspension of our stress response.

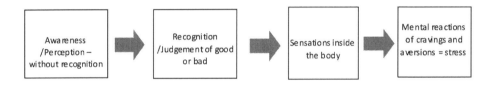

Becoming less judgemental can help us achieve a state of equanimity. When I say less judgemental I do not imply that judgements are not important and one can live without making judgements or decisions. It would be impossible to live without making judgements as every action requires judgement. Without making judgements we will not be able to carry out any action in a meaningful way.

Just as there is a time to act and there is a time to rest, there is also a time to judge and there is a time to stop judging. When we have worked hard during the day and feel tired, we come home and stop the actions; we put our feet up and allow our bodies to rest. In a similar fashion judgements are the actions of the mind and if we want to give rest to our mind we have to become less judgemental.

The next question that comes to mind is how does being less judgemental help us deal with our emotions?

If we look carefully, we will find that behind most stress reactions, maybe seven out of ten times, there is a judgement that we have made and emotions occur as a result of it. It could be a judgement that we have made now or in the past that triggered that emotion. Without judgement there will be no new emotions although one can experience a replay of old experiences that come up from the unconscious mind. For example, two people enter a room and see an object as a piece of rope and a snake respectively. The person who sees the object as a snake might experience an anxiety attack, whereas the person who sees it as a piece of rope will have no stress reaction. Neither of these two individuals knows the reality fully until they switch the light on. In this context the ability to suspend judgements until adequate information is available can be seen as a positive attribute.

We find ourselves in situations where our judgements are not needed, but we still keep on making judgements and most judgements are followed by certain emotions that can become a problem for us to deal with. We constantly make judgements about ourselves and others in terms of rich/poor, intelligent/stupid, beautiful/ugly, nice/nasty, and these judgements often go unchallenged.

The next question is how not to judge? One can adopt the following approaches with a view to achieving that end.

1. Understanding that most judgements that we make are based on incomplete information will help us understand the situation better. When we make judgements about people and situations, we do not know the inside stories of their lives.

   We might judge a neighbour as a "nasty person" based on how he behaved with somebody when we saw them; maybe he is a nice father or a nice husband. We get angry or annoyed at someone who is behaving unreasonably, but we do not know why he is doing so; maybe he has heard some bad news and is under stress.

2. All judgements are relative. We make judgements constantly in terms of rich/poor, intelligent/stupid, nice/nasty, beautiful/ugly, etc. about ourselves and about others. It's our emotions that make us see things in absolutistic terms (i.e. black and white whereas the reality lies somewhere in the middle, in the grey zone).

I can say to myself that I am intelligent, but compared to many people I am not that intelligent and I can say to myself that I am stupid, but compared to a lot of other people I am not that stupid. I can say to myself I am rich, but compared to a lot of other people I am not that rich and I can say to myself that I am poor, but then once again compared to a lot of people I am not that poor. Understanding the relative nature of our day-to-day judgements might help us move closer to the reality and achieve an equanimous mental state.

3. We tend to make global judgements when they should be situation-specific. The common judgements in this regard are describing people as un/supportive, un/friendly, etc. It is better to say that on this occasion this person behaved in a selfish or unfriendly manner, but in the past they behaved differently and things could be different in the future. Cultural stereotypes can also be understood in terms of global judgements we make about certain communities and judge individuals on that basis.

4. The outcome of our judgement is not known. What we judge as a bad situation might turn out to be a good one in the long run and what appears to be good might turn out to be just the opposite. Having a long-term perspective in mind might help us stay grounded in an equanimous mental state.

Painful experiences do as much good, if not more, as the pleasurable experiences. Shunning them will deprive us of at least half of all the opportunities for growth and development.

When my judgements went wrong

My poverty made me virtuous and money corrupted me.
My enemies helped me become stronger, and my friends accepted me and allowed me to stay weak.
My sorrows made me wiser and my happiness stagnated my growth.
My children saw my discipline as a form of control and not controlling them as lack of care.

My friends saw my tolerance as lack of ambition and my ambition as
a compensation for some deficiency in my personality.

Non-identification

Is this my real self?

I am the owner, my mind the pet
I am the sky, my thoughts are the clouds
I am the water, my worries are the impurities
I am the driver and my body and mind are the vehicle
I am the computer, my depression and anxiety are the software
I am the house, my fears are the guests who will stay for a while
I am the tree and my fantasies are the birds perching on them
I am the cloth, my emotions are the dirt and grease
I am the air, my desires are the storms

How can I believe in my thoughts, they are saying different things at different times, sometimes just the opposite. Surely all my thoughts can't be true. How do I know which ones are my real thoughts and which ones just random ruminations or wild thoughts?

I need to know which thoughts I should take seriously and which ones to discard. Am I identifying with the wrong thoughts and becoming their advocate without questioning them? Am I discarding my real thoughts that I should be guided by?

Answers to these questions can help us manage our stress better and for that we need to understand the process of identification.

The principle of non-identification might be a bit difficult to understand as it encourages us not to identify with our own thoughts and emotions. Our minds have the capacity to think of anything (i.e. the most improbable and absurd thoughts and thoughts that are totally alien to our personality). There is evidence for this from our dreams, which are part of our minds, but quite often we fail to make sense of them or understand them in terms of our normal day-to-day life.

This ability of the mind to think of anything has its own advantages and disadvantages.

Firstly, it helps us deal with all of the probable dangerous and fearful situations that might arise.

Secondly, it helps us to be more creative and think of the most improbable scenarios. The downside of this is that it can bring to the mind a lot of dreadful emotions and feelings and, if we are not careful, we start identifying with these thoughts and feelings and acting on them.

It might be easier to understand non-identification if we discussed the concept of identification first in some detail here. Identification is adopting something from outside and making it a part of our own thinking and personality.

Children, when growing up, adopt thoughts, emotions, values, posture, mannerisms and even voice from their parents without questioning or challenging them, and they become a part of their personality. This process is called identification or introjections, as the introjects originally came from outside and became part of oneself. This process of identification does not stop when a child becomes an adult, but continues throughout life. We adopt ideas and feelings from outside all the time and this has its own advantages and disadvantages.

The opposite of it can be described as dis-identification or non-identification, which can be of therapeutic value in coping with stress.

I normally ask clients to understand their minds in terms of the experience of being in a supermarket. When we walk into a supermarket with a trolley we see lots of things on the shelves. Just because we can see them does not mean that they belong to us. They will belong to us only when we pick up a product, go to the check-out and pay for it. In a similar fashion thousands of thoughts enter our mind every day. Just because a thought is in our mind does not mean it belongs to us. It will belong to us when we say yes to the thought and express an intention to act on it.

A lot of the time, thoughts are induced in our minds from outside and they do not truly belong to us; for example, someone sees a product in a shop that they want to buy, but on second thought realise that they already have a lot of similar items at home that they have never used. What is happening here is that we first identify with the thought and want to buy it, and later on stop this identification and decide not to act on it. Not buying the product is a result of our dis-identification from the desire to buy it.

In a similar fashion one can see that thoughts are often induced in our minds either from the environment or from our own unconscious mind and these thoughts do not truly represent our personality, needs and desires. It is therefore important to analyse our thoughts and feelings that truly belong to us and the thoughts and feelings that have either come from the outside world or from the unconscious mind that may not belong to us.

Clients who suffer from obsessive-compulsive disorder, psychotic episodes, sexual addictions, etc. find this non-identification principle helpful. I encourage them to understand these thoughts in terms of a spillage from the unconscious mind, very much like the oil spillage from the BP drilling station in the Gulf of Mexico recently.

Byron Katie (2002) has recently described a way of not believing in our thoughts by way of challenging each of our thoughts and asking ourselves the following four questions:

1. Is this thought true?
2. Am I 100% sure that this thought is true?
3. What are the consequences for me if I believe in this thought?
4. What are the consequences for me if I do not believe in this thought?

Dwelling on all the possible answers to these questions can help us tease out unrealistic thoughts from the realistic ones.

The next question that comes to mind is why in the first place somebody would identify with a thought that does not belong to them.

The answer is that in states of high anxiety or depression the emotion can get attached to an innocuous thought. We often find ourselves having thoughts that do not really belong to us in certain extreme situations (i.e. when going on high-rise buildings and when we look down, it is natural for someone to have the thought, "What if I jump from the window or fall down?" Or if one is driving fast on the motorway the thought comes, "What if a crash happens?") Now these thoughts are induced because of the nature of the external situation and one does not truly believe that these can happen in the normal course of life. In the normal course one will not see these thoughts as reflecting their true self. An anxious person's mind, which already has several negative emotions that are detached from their original context in the past, will find it easy to attach these thoughts to this new situation in order to make sense of them. The anxious person will therefore start identifying with these thoughts and will stop driving on motorways or going on high-rise buildings, assuming that it will make the anxiety go away. However, in normal course the individual who has these thoughts learns not to identify with them.

We are *not* the emotions

It is important to make a distinction between our real emotions that truly belong to us and the adopted ones. Some of these adopted emotions come to our mind like guests, but take control of the house and start dictating to us. We find ourselves pushed into a corner and becoming a slave to them. Quite a few of these emotions do not agree with our better judgement and we cannot shake them off.

Emotions can come from a number of different sources over which we have little control. They can come from our physiology or physical body, e.g. rapid heart rate causing anxiety or increased hormone levels causing depression, etc. At times emotions are like knee-jerk reactions to events that are happening outside our control (i.e. witnessing a trauma can cause shock or horror). The external situations can also lure us into believing in something that we do not clearly agree with, e.g. buying things that we do not really need.

In a similar fashion we find that emotions are produced instantaneously when we encounter a given situation (i.e. see, smell or hear something, etc.) and if we are not careful these emotions get hold of our attention and consciousness and become a part of ourselves. All this happens as a result of identification with a particular emotion.

It is easier to deal with an emotion whilst it is in our conscious mind. Once it goes into the unconscious mind we have little control over it and what happens to it further on depends upon what sort of environment there is inside the unconscious mind.

We find that many of these emotions are deeply buried in our consciousness, but they still do not really belong to us. It can be explained further by giving the example of dirty linen. The dirt and grease in dirty clothes go deep into the fabric, but don't belong there and can be separated. In a similar fashion depression or anxiety can go deep inside the mind, but they can be separated very much like the dirt in the linen. They belong to us for as long as we identify with them and act on their behalf rather than acting against them.

The principle of impermanence

It helps to be mindful of the fact that everything that exists in the material world is temporary and the same principle applies to our mind as well. Every thought and feeling has a time span and sooner or later it comes to an end. No matter how painful or distressing a thought is, it will not stay in the mind forever. A constant awareness of it is helpful.

The same principle also applies to good feelings and thoughts. No matter how enjoyable a good thought is, it cannot stay in the mind forever. Applying this principle to everyday life can help us achieve a state of neutrality of the mind. Whatever is intolerable might become tolerable when we see it in the light of impermanence.

Simply saying to ourselves that a given thought, emotion or the situation that we are in is temporary will not make it disappear instantly. But the chain reaction of judgements and emotions that normally starts soon after perceiving something can be worked on better if we keep in mind the impermanent nature of things. A part of our mind stops reacting to the thought or the situation when we see it in the light of impermanence and then it becomes easier to handle.

In a similar fashion when we apply this principle to the good things in life, they will not disappear just because we have thought about them as impermanent. They will only go when their time comes, but we can enjoy their presence much more if we can visualise their temporary nature.

The experience of impermanence can make us more tolerant, more humane, kinder and more generous to others as well as to ourselves.

Some clients ask me, "Is it not scary to think that way?" My answer to them is, "Yes, it is the possibility of death that is scary, not thinking about it, and in that respect we are all in the same boat. It's very much like there is a bull in the room and no one is talking about it. What is scary here is the presence of the bull, not talking about it. It might help us make the bull (or death) less scary if we talked about it."

Some clients worry that they will become depressed if they think that all good things will come to an end. I ask them to be mindful of the fact that today we have the good things and we can enjoy them more if we thought about their temporariness.

Another advantage in thinking this way is that one can become desensitised to thoughts of loss and separation, which are inevitable, and this desensitisation is a very important milestone in one's psychological growth.

Death anxiety is the mother of all anxieties and it underlies many of the psychiatric symptoms such as panic attacks, agoraphobia, paranoid thoughts, etc. When one has worked on death anxiety, a lot of psychological symptoms automatically disappear.

How to practise the principle of impermanence

I normally ask clients to buy sticky coloured dots (they can be any colour, yellow, green, blue) and stick them everywhere in their surroundings – on the car dashboard, kitchen table, computer, desk, their wallet, laptop, mobile phone, etc. Whenever they see the dot they are to say to themselves, "The situation I am in is temporary, the meeting I am having with this person right now is temporary, the thought that I have right now in my mind is temporary, the emotion I have in my heart is temporary." Alternatives to the dots could be wearing a ring or keeping an object in their pockets that can serve as a reminder to this principle.

This principle might enable clients to deal with the situation they are confronted with more appropriately. I encourage clients to apply the same principle to their symptoms as well. If they are having a good day and are free from their anxiety and depression they are to say to themselves, "Hold on, it may be temporary and in a few hours' or a few days' time the symptoms may return." By doing so they are preparing themselves for a situation when symptoms might come back and if they do, they are able to deal with the recurrence more effectively. When this happens, they once again try to understand them in terms of impermanence.

Sometimes clients have the expectation that as soon as they say that the symptom is temporary, then it will disappear. The symptom may or may not disappear immediately, but it stops the individual from getting more anxious and depressed as a result of having the symptom. It breaks the vicious cycle that puts one on a negative spiral. By doing this, a part of one's mind is freed from the emotion and can get on with everyday business.

Writing an emotion diary

We experience thousands of emotions and thoughts on a daily basis and they tend to slip in and out of our consciousness on a continual basis. Many of these are forgotten or pushed into the unconscious mind soon after experiencing them. They generally do not stay long enough in our consciousness for us to understand their significance and impact on us. Thoughts and emotions that are forgotten cannot be worked on; therefore it would be desirable to put them down on a piece of paper so that they can get worked on.

Writing down the emotions that we experience on a daily basis in a journal can help us manage them better, very much like writing down the details of our income and expenses can help us manage our finances better.

The emotions and thoughts that we experience vary from time to time and are at times quite opposite to each other, creating confusion as to which ones should be taken seriously. For example, in the morning, we believe that a particular person is a friend and after a few hours or days we might perceive the same person as unfriendly. It is important to work out which of these emotions and thoughts represent our true selves and which ones are unrealistic and need to be ignored.

I generally ask clients to start writing how different situations make them feel and to convert their emotions into language. It is important to write something on a regular basis and read what one has written at least twice a week and to destroy the notes that are more than four weeks old. It means that you are not writing for posterity and no one has access to your journal. It is only for one's own use. Writing in this manner can act as a mirror to one's own mind because we can't inspect our emotions properly whilst we are inside them as these emotions colour our perception. We can make better sense of these emotions if we examine them when we are out of them.

Some clients come and tell me that when they start reading their own thoughts they can see very clearly that the thought was not realistic as it appears alien to them after a while. This helps clients label quite a few of their thoughts as unrealistic and these thoughts have a tendency to recur. Clients therefore are able to spot these thoughts easily and early on next time when they occur. Writing down the thoughts therefore helps clients fine tune them.

Some clients might find that writing about a particularly traumatic experience makes them feel worse as the experience grows on them. If that were true for them then they should start writing down their pleasant experiences and good memories as well, and by the same principle the positive emotions should also start growing.

It is important to note that revisiting old experiences can become problematic when one doesn't know how to deal with them. However, if someone is already in therapy and is learning how to deal with these experiences they find that by writing things down they are able to work through them better.

CHAPTER 9

Recovery Process

"Magical cures can disappear magically."

In the beginning there was an idea
And then an intention
And then a decision, followed by an action
And then there were problems and the experience of failure
Followed by loss of motivation
And then there was a phase of no action, and return to old habits
And then there was experience of more suffering
And then there was a renewed motivation and action
And then there was a small taste of success
And then there was more action, and perseveration
And then there was more success and some failures
And then there was much more success and very little failure

If I count the number of failures, they were greater than the number
of successes
But I have arrived at my destination and
I am happy

Prochaska et al (1992) have described the above stages of change that a client goes through during recovery from addictive behaviours but their model seems to have a wider applicability. Recovery from a psychological problem is never smooth and predictable. There are a number of factors that play a role in reaching the goal of freedom from symptoms. Neither the client nor the therapist is fully aware of the obstacles in the way, as quite a few of them operate at the unconscious level. Secondly, it's difficult to judge the improvement by taking into consideration only the feeling state of a client at a given point in time. The intensity of feelings at a given point in time can be misleading.

Are You Inside an Emotion or Outside of It?

The same reality hurts very badly at one time, but we can put up with it at other times; why is this so? Perhaps we move in and out of the emotion without being aware or having an intention to do so.

A client came to me after attending a few therapy sessions and said that he was back to square one, as the night before he was feeling exactly the same as he felt when he started the therapy sessions. I asked him how long the feeling lasted. He said about an hour, which was slightly less than the duration he used to remain unwell for before. His worry was that the intensity of his feeling was the same. I asked him to visualise a journey between two cities, which involved crossing five tunnels. When one is crossing the last tunnel, maybe after driving a 100-mile stretch, the experience of being inside a tunnel can be exactly the same as when one is crossing the first tunnel. The darkness and the scariness of being inside a tunnel. Someone who is not mindful might think he is back to square one.

When you are inside a particular emotion you are likely to lose objectivity. Emotions make us think in absolutistic terms; things are black or white, there are no grey zones. When we deal with emotions the yardstick of progress in the initial stages should not be the intensity of our feelings but whether we know how to deal with them and feel able to do so. The real progress happens in small chunks, bit by bit, and the journey is very long. Magical cures can disappear magically. One has to work hard with oneself and against oneself. There are no external enemies on this path of behaviour change and personal development.

Secondly, changing one's mind requires disagreeing with oneself, hence one needs a sounding board or a therapist who can act as a mirror to one's mind. In addition to other things, therapy also involves confronting one's own inner mind, which can be a stressful experience. This confronting can sometimes reactivate symptoms that outwardly appear to be in remission.

It is important to understand that experiencing a symptom in a controlled setting can be an opportunity to work on it as this feeling can't be worked on when it is buried deep in the unconscious mind. As they say, the cure of pain lies in the pain; running away from it would be running away from the cure.

There Is Always a Hope for Everyone

The concept of hope is always linked with its object: hope for what. When it comes to improvement in psychological health (i.e. moving on from where one is), there is always hope for betterment, no matter how incurable the disease is. Even terminally ill people who can't be cured of their ailment and death is inevitable for them can be made to feel better with psychological interventions. Psychotherapy is therefore a panacea for all problems. However, if one is looking at complete cure from a particular disease, psychotherapy may not achieve that goal for some disorders and has to be seen as an adjunct treatment.

Why Do We Seek Help?

It is not for the abnormal behavior per se that we seek help, but the problem it creates for us. Once the problem is resolved the motivation to seek help drops and one drops out of treatment, even though the behaviour persists. At times we find that clients have achieved a comfort level with their symptoms that they are familiar with. Any change, even if it is for betterment, can create uncertainty that comes with confronting an unknown. A known devil is better than the unknown ones.

There are two main reasons why people come for help; firstly, when they encounter an unpleasant and humiliating experience; secondly, the lure of a better life that is possible when symptoms disappear. The first reason leads to drastic actions, but there is a greater risk of relapse as it may be a knee jerk reaction to a humiliating experience. While the second one is a weak motivating factor initially, it can work slowly and steadily, and the recovery achieved may be longer lasting.

The Role of Discipline

Without discipline we are like a rudderless ship that is at the mercy of the gales and may never reach its destination. It's important during the recovery process that we make certain rules and live by them. Nobody else can make those rules for us, as we know our limits well and also know how much those limits can be pushed safely in order to achieve the desired results. The rules should make us push our boundaries a little bit, but not too much, and we should keep revising the rules if they are not working or are too difficult to follow. For example, someone who is addicted to alcohol can make rules for not drinking on certain days, at certain times, in certain situations, or not beyond a certain number of drinks a day, etc.

How Long Will the Recovery Phase Last?

Once you start on the journey for behaviour change it's a life-long process. The recovery happens in the reverse fashion to the appearance of symptoms. The problems that appeared last are likely to go first and the ones that came first will go in the end. But one should be able to notice a change with every step one takes. The duration of therapy doesn't matter as long as one notices improvement with every step one takes, as sooner or later one will reach the goal. If one is carrying a burden of fifty kilos on his head, with some intervention it can be reduced to forty-five kilos in a month's time and to forty kilos in another month; it's worthwhile seeking that intervention, as there is hope that one day all the burden will be lifted.

In the early stages change may not happen in the form of removal of symptoms, but it should be evident in one's ability to deal with them effectively. At times one ends up feeling worse soon after the start of therapy, which may be related to getting in touch with the inner distress that needs to be worked on. One should see this as an opportunity to work on those deeper issues that would not have surfaced otherwise to get worked on.

From Stress to Being Supernatural

We find that people who get out of poverty by working hard don't stop at being average earners. They continue to use the skills they have acquired to make money and end up being rich. The same principle applies to the recovery from stress and psychological symptoms. Once a client becomes skilful in dealing with their emotions and comes out of their illnesses, they have the option to carry on working on their emotions with the objective of dealing with the normal human suffering. This endeavour provides immunity to further stress and they can acquire superhuman abilities in dealing with life stress.

The Role of Medication

When my depression started my doctor wanted me to take
antidepressants and I didn't want them.
But now he wants me to stop it and I can't do without them.

Those who take medication for their psychological problems often ask themselves if they have become addicted to the prescription medication. Before trying to answer this question one needs to understand the difference between addiction and therapeutic use.

The word addiction means inappropriate or excessive use of something, such as a drug, when it is not indicated. Therapeutic use, on the other hand, means using the drug to relieve clinical symptoms even though it is long-term use, such as use of insulin for diabetes. However, excessive reliance on medication can also eventually lead to addiction.

For the majority of psychological problems, apart from chronic psychotic illnesses where long-term drug use is indicated, psychotherapy can work as well as drugs. But in initial stages, if the problem is of moderate severity, it's best to use a combination of drugs and psychotherapy for a greater efficacy of this combination. But in the longer term, attempt should be made to manage them only through psychological means. Very much like bone injury requiring the use of crutches in the initial stages, but a regular course of physiotherapy can make them unnecessary in the longer term. Drugs are therefore needed as crutches in the initial stages. However, if the problem is of a mild nature, then attempts should first be made to treat it with psychotherapy only, rather than rushing for drugs.

During the process of recovery one goes through several phases, such as uninformed optimism, informed pessimism, informed optimism and eventual recovery. It's therefore important to know at what stage of recovery one is, so that one can work in accordance with the needs of one's recovery process.

CHAPTER 10

Spirituality: The Fourth Dimension of Life

"He who considers himself free is free indeed;
he who considers himself bound remains bound."

Spiritual person: a definition

He is happy when he is with people and happy when he is alone.
He is happy when he is busy and happy when he has nothing much to do.
He is happy when others care about him and happy when they ignore him.
He doesn't wish he had a different set of friends, relatives and family.
He can enjoy all the pleasures of life knowing full well that this enjoyment will end one day.
He is neither afraid of dying, nor is he fed up of living.
He is not afraid of his superiors and doesn't try to please them.
He doesn't boss about his subordinates as he doesn't enjoy being a boss.
He neither lives in the past nor in the future.

He doesn't wish he had a different past, as he can see how much he has learnt from his mistakes and unpleasant experiences.

He is not afraid of his future as he knows that the best is yet to come, but doesn't resent his present circumstances.

He is happy when he is able to help people and happy when he has nothing to give.

He is happy when he sees people happy and compassionate when he sees them unhappy.

He has no desire to travel more and see more of this world, but at the same time doesn't mind it if the situation demands.

He isn't looking for miracles as he knows that everything in this world, including his own existence, is a miracle.

He is willing to wait for things until the time is right, as he knows that things happen only when the time is right.

He is willing to live with uncertainty and expects the unexpected, as he knows that this is what human life is about.

He doesn't feel guilty about not being able to give more than what he has got to his children.

His friendly feelings towards his fellow beings is unbroken and unbreakable.

He doesn't expect anything from anyone, but accepts help when offered.

Do we really need spirituality?

The answer to that question is "no" if we are talking of the short term, but in the longer term we can't live a happy life without bringing in elements of spirituality into our life. We may not be aware of the spiritual elements that are already there in our lives and just see them as requirements of a good life. Whereas many of us who call ourselves spiritual may, in fact, be worldly people seeking power, glory, fame, riches and other worldly things in the guise of spiritual growth.

We don't need spirituality if the external world as we see it was enough to bring about lasting happiness. Unfortunately, that is not the case; there is an element of unsatisfactoriness built into human life and that is why we live on hopes and not on what we already have.

Before we go any further in trying to understand whether we need spirituality or not, we need to understand what spirituality is and how much of it we are already practising, as it has been understood differently in different cultures and at different times in history.

In ancient times spirituality was practised in the guise of philosophy, religion or simple mainstream education that was imparted in schools. In ancient India all children were sent to live with their teacher's families in residential units called Gurukul Kangri so that they could learn spiritual values among other skills of life. In some cultures no distinction was made between religion and spirituality, as religion offered people a valid route to practise what can now be described as spiritual practices.

There are a number of different ways of understanding spirituality as described here:

- Purification or perfection of one's consciousness or "Being".
- Inner journey enabling a person to discover the essence of their being.
- Matters relating to one's immaterial reality (what cannot be perceived through the five senses, but exists and influences us).
- Being connected to a larger reality or infinite, which is beyond ourselves. The transpersonal aspects of our existence that connect us to other beings and the infinite universe.
- A path to the higher states of awareness.

In modern times the attention has shifted from religion to spirituality, but science is still divorced from both these approaches as the methods of enquiry are different. However, historically the treatment of mental illnesses has been the concern of a number of different fields, such as religion, spirituality, philosophy, music, art, literature, etc., and it was brought into the medical fold only about a hundred years ago.

Psychiatry has grown and gained legitimacy as a scientific discipline as a result of its adherence to what is understood as neuroscience, but something appears to have been lost in the process. Human existence is not just a scientific problem, hence restricting ourselves to science is going to limit us. The boundaries of science are expanding and they are claiming ground from spirituality and charting uncharted territories of the mind. A deeper understanding of spirituality therefore offers a peep into the future of science.

Religion v spirituality

Religion and spirituality are different in that religion is man-made whereas spirituality is universal and natural. Religion makes us see the differences between different individuals whereas spirituality looks at the common ground between individuals. In spite of this difference there is a big overlap between the two.

Both religion and spirituality are concerned with issues that are beyond the material and the social world. They are also concerned with man's relationship with himself and the infinite/God. When we look at the common ground between the two, spirituality can be seen as the essence of religion and religion as the outer wrappings of spirituality.

The scientific approach in its current incarnation appears to be limited as it reduces the human experience to certain biological and biochemical reactions that could be studied in laboratories. It focuses mainly on what can be objectivised and repeated in test situations, the rules that generally do not apply to the mind entirely. It would be fair to say that medicine is ethnocentric; anything that cannot be understood using the current scientific paradigms is discarded as unscientific and therefore not worthy of attention.

It appears that, in the field of psychiatry, the attempts to explain all human behaviour in terms of biochemical reactions have not been successful and a lot of human experience remains beyond the reach of scientific understanding. Secondly, it may not be desirable to reduce all human experience to neural impulses and hormonal changes.

These problems can be solved only if the scientific methods could be refined further to confront new challenges. Spirituality appears to offer a direction in which psychiatry can expand its boundaries.

Solitude: a precondition for spiritual experience

Just as the body needs a break from its actions in order to recover from tiredness and the mind needs a break from the thoughts and emotions to recover its strength, the consciousness also needs a break from the perceptions of the external world and the judgements of oneself, in order to get connected with inner joys and the infinite.

This turning in of the consciousness into itself and rejoicing in itself is the purpose of any spiritual exercise and it generally happens only during periods of solitude. Solitude therefore is essential for spiritual growth and development. Seeking solitude in this context cannot be seen as an escape from the reality of the external world, but as facing one's inner reality. In fact, our involvement with the distractions of the external world can be seen as an escape from oneself.

Solitude is therefore the first necessary step in the direction of inner healing. Unfortunately, many of us find solitude painful or distressing, mainly because we haven't worked on the inner negative experiences that come in the way of getting connected with the inner positive experiences, the ocean of primordial consciousness. Solitude is necessary even for undoing the negative feelings as worldly distraction generally doesn't help us undo them.

Positive feelings generally do not undo negative feelings; they only suppress them. At most they give us strength to face the negative. If we want to get rid of the negative feelings they have to be dealt with on their own terms. Solitude is one of the more powerful ways of undoing the negative feelings, as one is not seeking positive feelings during periods of solitude but tries to reflect on what is already there in the mind. It is therefore important that for short periods of time we disengage ourselves from social ties and try to be on our own.

Some clients report that their initial experience of being on their own had been frightening. This is probably because they experience a sense of losing their normal identities that are so tied up with something or the other in the outer world.

This turning in often produces anxiety. However, if the anxiety can be tolerated, seeking solitude can lead to unfolding of new inner capabilities.

In modern times Anthony Storr (1997), a psychiatrist and a psychotherapist, has argued in his book entitled *Solitude* that the capacity to be alone is also an aspect of emotional maturity. He further states that in a culture in which interpersonal relationships are generally considered to provide the answer to every form of distress, it is difficult to persuade well-meaning helpers that solitude can be as therapeutic as emotional support (Storr, 1997).

He further argues that individuals who do not have strong spiritual connections with their own souls and the supernatural tend to idealise interpersonal relationships and marriage and as a result look upon these relationships as the principal source of happiness. This overvaluation of relationships may result in their break up – a malady of modern times.

Therapeutic benefits of spiritual practices

Science grew as a revolt against religion and as a result religion stopped being a subject matter of study for science. It is only recently that science turned its attention to religious and spiritual practices and found the therapeutic elements in there. Spiritual values seem to be helpful when it comes to managing one's own stress.

The spiritual values

The commonly understood spiritual values are acceptance, truthfulness, authenticity, detachment, forgiveness, surrender, love, moderation in sensual gratification, transcendence, etc. There is no need to make a conscious effort to practise all of these values; practising any one of these to the extreme is enough for enlightenment as practising one automatically leads to the others.

Acceptance

I came across a poem on a wall poster at a friend's house in India about thirty years ago (author unknown). It was about accepting one's physical attributes and social circumstances. I have expanded the idea further to include mental attributes and emotions as well.

I Accept, Fully Accept

I accept:

> *My ethnic background, my community.*
> *My appearance with all its imperfections; my hair, my face, the colour of my skin.*
> *My parents, my partner, my children and my relatives.*
> *My work, my colleagues, my friends and my neighbours.*
> *My poverty and my riches.*

My talents and my handicaps.
My past and what future has in store for me.

I accept, fully accept:

My mind with all its mood swings.
My desires, dreams, fears, frustrations, worries, depression, etc.
My successes and my failures.
I accept all that life has to give and I can also accept the possibility of death.

This acceptance should not be seen as the end point for someone who feels helpless in the face of difficulties, but the starting point for bringing about a positive change in one's life. Non-acceptance of things is a form of mental reaction that consumes a lot of energy and blocks growth, whereas acceptance releases a lot of energy that can enable us to change things.

It is possible to reverse the age-old saying:

"God give me the strength to accept the things I cannot change, the courage to change the things I can, and to know the difference between the two."

The new saying would be something like this:

"I accept everything and after that try to change certain things I can for better and finally choose the best."

In my opinion acceptance of things does not mean you should not try to change for better. A constant effort to accept and also to work towards betterment should be our motto.

A client of mine was very upset about his son's behaviour, which was not out of the ordinary for an adolescent boy, and told me that he couldn't accept what his son was doing. My answer to him was, "That's fine, but can you accept the fact that you can't accept your son's behaviour as of now and it may be that this state of your mind and your son's behaviour are also temporary, so not going to last very long?" The thought that everything is temporary can make us accept things that we find unacceptable in the first place.

I haven't been fair to myself

*My eyes wanted to see Swiss Alps and I closed my eyes to the beautiful
meadows in front of me; I haven't been fair to my eyes.
I wanted to smell roses and I threw the marigold flowers away in the
bin; I haven't been fair to my nose.
I wanted to eat the finest Belgian chocolates and I spat out the
delicious toffee pudding; I haven't been fair to my tongue.
I wanted to listen to Mozart and turned a deaf ear to the beautiful
country music playing in the room; I haven't been fair to my ears.
I wanted someone to love me madly and didn't see that madness in
my beloved; I haven't been fair to my heart.
I wanted to become a perfect human being and ignored all the
opportunities to become a real human being.
I haven't been fair to myself.*

Truthfulness

*Accepting the truth is stressful in the short term; not accepting it is
stressful in the longer term.*

Truth is a strong antidote to almost all psychiatric disorders, although in the short term it can be the cause of our stress. The Bible says follow the truth and truth will liberate you and this seems to connect with how mental illness is produced. Most psychiatric symptoms arise as a result of our attempts to distort the reality that is unacceptable to us. The exaggeration of truth will also fall in the category of distorting it as the truth here *as it is* is not acceptable to us.

At times I see myself covering up truths, but the truth has a way of slipping out in public view in spite of all my attempts. I therefore made a rule a few years ago that I would not regret or get upset about people knowing things about me if what has become known to others is a truth about myself, as it would have happened in the future; it is good that it has happened now so that I can put the fear of it becoming public behind me.

Authenticity

At a very simple level authenticity means being genuine and real rather than artificial and phoney. What is outside is inside. In existentialism, authenticity is the degree to which one is true to one's own personality, spirit and character, despite external pressures.

An inauthentic person tries to be a certain kind of person they are not and therefore has a need to distort their true inner and outer realities. This inability to accept the reality leads to efforts to distort it, which is the bedrock of a lot of psychological problems. If one looks carefully, almost all psychiatric symptoms and psychological defence mechanisms are about distortion of reality. And if distortion of reality is the problem, then authenticity is the antidote. In this respect, being truthful and honest can prevent and cure a lot of psychological problems. Vipassana meditation is all about being authentic; the very definition of Vipassana is "to see the reality as it is" and in order to do that one has to walk on the path of authenticity.

Detachment and Freedom

> *Find something in you that is not affected by pleasure and pain, having or not having, being or not being.*

The first questions that spring to mind after hearing the word detachment are, "What's the need? What's wrong with attachments to things and this world?"

The simple answer to this is that there is nothing wrong with being attached to things and people if separation from them is not a possibility. But unfortunately, every good thing or relationship has to come to an end and the stronger the attachment, the greater is the suffering. Separation and loss are inevitable. There is an element of unsatisfactoriness built in to human life and things around us. Attachment to things is bondage and detachment is freedom. It would be wrong to assume that being detached will kill our enjoyment of things and relationships. On the contrary it enhances the enjoyment as one doesn't take things for granted and tries to make the most of them knowing full well the possibility of separation.

Modern psychology has devoted a lot of attention to the study of attachment theories and classified different types of attachment problems that can explain psychiatric symptoms, but there is hardly any talk of the concept of detachment and how it can help us prevent stress.

According to the spiritual traditions it is a bondage when the mind desires or grieves anything, rejects or accepts anything, feels happy or angry at anything. It is liberation when the mind is detached from all sense experiences.

Getting too involved in worldly affairs can be a cause of stress. I say to my clients that at least a part of your psyche should not get entangled in the worldly affairs – whether you are making enough money or not, whether your plans are heading in the right direction or not, whether you are in good health or not, etc.

Spirituality helps us develop a sense of detachment to things that we can perceive through our five senses, so that we can address the commonly neglected human concerns of a transcendental nature.

This detachment does not mean a lack of caring and loving feelings towards our fellow beings, but not losing sight of the existential reality of one's aloneness in the end.

A detached person loves and provides care exactly like an attached person, maybe better, but this endeavour doesn't result in personal suffering; very much like the love and care provided by a nanny, which is not less than that provided by a mother in any way, but when it comes to an end there is no personal suffering.

A sense of detachment can be cultivated by means of witnessing our emotions in a non-reacting manner, discussed elsewhere in this book.

I feel free when

People are selfish and indifferent to me, as I can also justify the gaps in my caring for them.
They can't feel my pain, as it takes away the possibility of inflicting it on them.
Things change, as it breaks my attachment to them.
My possessions are threatened, as they also occupy a space in my mind.
I lose money, as the experience teaches me to be less reliant on it.

People don't bother to call, as it gives me time to complete the tasks
imposed upon me from within.
I think of death, as it reduces my fear of it.
I work for work's sake and not for any gains, as it makes me less insecure.
I don't need anything from anybody, as I become immune to stress.

Forgiveness

I am not perfect; how can I expect others to be perfect?

There have been times when I forgave people, but Mother Nature chose not to forgive them; they had to face the consequences of their actions irrespective of whether I forgave them or not. But one thing that always happened (i.e. every time I forgave someone) was I felt better within myself. There must be laws of psyche that determine what should be the consequences of one's actions. I have therefore developed a faith in the superordinate systems, the higher intelligence or the laws of psyche that are at work. Having faith in them and surrendering to them helps me relieve my stress, as I no longer have the need to see the justice being done; I know it will be done.

Surrender

I can take pride in the fact that I am controlling my life to a great extent, but a careful thought would indicate that, for that to happen, nature has created some mechanisms by which I am able to exercise that control. For example, I can lift my right hand at will, but I can do so only because dozens of chemicals are released in my brain and in the muscles and nerves of my shoulder and arm in very minute quantities at precise moments, yet I am not even aware of the names of these chemicals, let alone the ability to manufacture them or regulate their release. I can light a candle with a match-stick, but that will happen only when there is oxygen in the room, which I have not created and couldn't create even if I wanted to.

Psychologists tell us that the unconscious mind is the more intelligent side of our personality, which is at work all of the time without our knowledge. A higher intelligence seems to be at work that supports our life on this planet. Surrendering oneself to that higher force or supra-ordinate forces can be helpful. Even when things do not seem to be going in the right direction, having trust in the laws of psyche or higher forces can be helpful. Very much like a child who trusts his mother and listens to her even when she is suggesting things contrary to his wishes. It is the act of surrender that helps more than the object of it, as one learns to let go of things that can be stressful.

Love

Love is the solvent in which stress dissolves.

A spiritual person loves everyone the way a mother loves her only child. Trying to hold on to the feelings of love in the face of adversity helps us confront the whole gamut of our negative emotions that get worked on. I have chosen not to dwell on this topic here as it is more than adequately covered by scholars in texts that are easily available. My attempts to do so would be like lighting a candle in a well-lit room.

Non-Doer-Ship

Those who believe in God find it easy to see themselves as an instrument in the hands of God and they can see God's Will even in things that are happening contrary to their desires and they become more accepting of them. Whereas for others, it requires a certain amount of awareness of things that are happening outside of one's control and are supporting their lives on this planet. It is also about having faith in the laws of the universe, including the laws of psyche, and also having faith in one's own destiny. Not taking personal credit for things that happen through us frees us in some ways so that we drop our expectation of positive results happening as a result of our positive actions. It also takes away the unnecessary guilt that comes with brooding over one's actions.

I have seen from my personal experience that my intention to help people doesn't translate into actual help for them until and unless it is destined to happen. In a similar fashion, things happen through me quite effortlessly and with very little intention and effort when the time is right. How can I take full credit for those things? I can only take full credit for just having the intention to do certain things and allowing them to happen.

Introspection

Introspection can be described as consciousness turning inwards and there are four ways of doing it. These are reflecting one's consciousness onto one's thoughts, emotions, actions and inner body sensations. All four can be combined for a greater effectiveness. Modern science has used the first three as forms of therapy described as cognitive therapy, experiential therapies and behaviour therapy respectively. Meditative practices, such as mindfulness, use the fourth domain of sensations to reflect on one's inner being. This turning-in of the consciousness onto itself brings about spiritual joys and rapturous feelings incomparable to any worldly experience that one has had in their life.

It is very easy to talk about spiritual values and how they can help us reduce stress, but the difficult bit is how to develop those values, if they are missing from our lives. Is there a way to promote them? Vipassana meditation is one such way to achieve that.

Mindfulness Meditation

In a nutshell mindfulness is ***noticing more, judging less***. It is a method of awareness and introspection that involves a conscious attempt to focus attention intensely on the present moment, noting thoughts, feelings, perception, images and sensations without judging them, participating in them or acting on them. It is observation of the contents of our mind as they appear and disappear without reacting to them.

Mindfulness is not about changing our thoughts and emotions, but about relating to them differently.

Every thought and every emotion dies its natural death if we do not participate in them. Participation here means judging and emotionally reacting to them whilst experiencing them. The typical reactions that arise are those of craving for or aversion to things.

A detached observation, with suspended evaluations and mental reactions, does not encourage the suppression or expression of emotions, but allows observation with impartiality, making it possible for individuals to deal with these emotional reactions appropriately. It enables clients to become aware of experiences without being attached to them.

Mindfulness meditation enables individuals to enlarge their conscious awareness beyond their thoughts and feelings to include perception, sensation, images, drives, etc. The practice involves training of attention and its redeployment in ways that lead to improved concentration of mind and also unfolding of the unconscious mind.

What heals in mindfulness meditation:

- Living in the present moment
- Shifting attention from thoughts and feelings to perception and sensation
- Promotion of equanimity
- Neutralisation of the negative emotions
- Ability to generate positive emotions

Mindfulness has its roots in what Buddha taught some 2,500 years ago. It was taught by him as a universal remedy for all sorts of human suffering. In recent times mindfulness meditation has been used successfully in the treatment of clinical anxiety, chronic pain, addictive disorders (such as alcohol and drug dependence), binge-eating, smoking and psychosomatic illnesses.

Mindfulness meditation enables clients to transform their reactions (which are conditioned) into actions that are based on free choice. The central aim of mindfulness is to free individuals from the restricting influences of strong past emotions, both positive and negative.

Mindfulness meditation has been practised in the Eastern world for more than twenty-five centuries, but it's only recently that it has become popular in the West. The reasons for this could be many-fold.

- • Firstly, in Buddhist traditions, until recently, teachers were forbidden to teach this technique to householders as it was reserved only for the monks who chose to dedicate their whole lives to attaining spiritual goals. It was not taught to seekers who were not fully prepared and did not understand the value of it.
- • Secondly, in the last decade or so, the scientific community has become more open to the spiritual aspects of mental health. It may be that science has realised its limitations when dealing with the mind

as its subject matter and is looking to expand its boundaries by way of understanding mindfulness meditation.

Mindfulness meditation is based on the assumption that our minds have a natural ability to undo stress and this ability is regulated by certain homeostatic mechanisms. These mechanisms are activated during meditation as individuals get connected with their inner state of affairs by way of becoming aware of their inner body sensations. For example, they become aware of their emotions long before they arrive on the conscious plane. Mindfulness, therefore, acts at precognitive or unconscious levels. It also helps clients deal with their strong emotions by using certain cognitive strategies (i.e. understanding all experiences in terms of transitoriness and not identifying with them). This allows clients to become detached from the goings-on in their minds, thereby enabling them to manage these emotions better.

Vipassana Meditation

Vipassana is an intensive form of mindfulness meditation. The term Vipassana means "to see things as they really are and not as they appear to be". Our habitual ways of understanding the world tend to be coloured by our past conditionings and very often we fail to see others' points of view. It may be desirable to integrate the multiplicity of perspectives in order to arrive at a better understanding of things. This is possible only when we have gained the ability to free (or distance) ourselves from our own fantasies and fears and reach a reasonable state of equanimity. It is assumed that the mind is at its best when it is equanimous.

Vipassana enables us to neutralise the restricting influences of our past experiences and attain greater equanimity. This helps in exercising a free choice.

Vipassana is not just a technique. It is a way of being in this world, although initially one has to employ a method or make preparations for the required change to occur. It is a return to our true, real nature, which we have forgotten.

No attempt is made to impose meanings from outside. The individual is encouraged to face anything that comes up in the mind, no matter how distressing, without any desire to distort it. Although no attempt is made to analyse the experience, one does use some understanding of certain universal principles, which are helpful in freeing oneself from past mental reactions, false beliefs and false self-definition.

All experiences are understood in terms of the following three principles:

1. **Anicca** (impermanence): Nothing is permanent; everything exists against the background of no-thingness, which is predominant. This leads to a state of unsatisfactoriness, which is at the bottom of human life, and one begins to question the essence of things.

2. **Anatta** (egolessness or non-identification): Not identifying oneself with what one encounters during introspection. It is not a denial or disowning of parts of ourselves, but recognition of false identifications and letting go of things that we are holding on to out of our own insecurities.

3. **Dukkha** (suffering): This is the corollary of impermanence. One can think of two different types of suffering: in-built and self-created. In-built suffering is not related to anything in particular. It is about eventual nothingness or uncertainty about things. In spite of our best efforts we remain subject to chance and battle with doubts about the fairness of human life. It is easier to avoid self-created suffering as it originates from our own mental reactions, self-definitions and the conclusions we draw about our experiences and the world in general. There is a link between the two types of sufferings. Our unwillingness to accept in-built suffering makes us react in certain ways, leading to further suffering. Vipassana encourages us to confront the ultimate concerns pertaining to in-built suffering. The "acceptance of suffering" in Buddhist psychology is generally misunderstood as a nihilistic approach. The acceptance should not be viewed as the end point. Rather, it is a means to achieving the goal of total eradication of suffering. Even in-built suffering dissolves with the dissolution of one's ego. It becomes a non-issue as one transcends the human ways of looking at things.

The ten-day course

The practice of Vipassana is divided into three parts, sila, samadhi and panna, being respectively morality, concentration and wisdom. Sila, or virtuous living, is the basis for samadhi (control of mind leading to one-pointedness). In turn, it is only when samadhi is attained that one can develop panna. Therefore, sila and samadhi are the prerequisites for panna. By panna is meant the understanding of annica, annata and dukkha, through the practice of Vipassana.

Students wishing to learn Vipassana undergo a minimum ten-day residential course, during which time they take the precepts not to kill, not to steal, not to commit sexual misconduct, not to speak lies and to refrain from intoxicants. These courses are conduced worldwide under the directions and guidance of Mr S. N. Goenka, the principle teacher in the tradition of Sayagi U Ba Khin. More details can be obtained from website www.dhamma.org. For the entire ten days they do little other than sleep, eat, meditate and wash. For the first three days, concentration of the mind is developed by observing the inhalation and exhalation of the breath and the consequent sensations that arise.

From the fourth day, students learn to feel sensations inside the body in order to awaken the insights related to the mind and matter. Each day's progress is explained during an hour's discourse in the evening. The course closes on the last day with the practice of loving kindness meditation, the sharing of the purity developed during the course with all beings.

Embodiment

Meditators in the tradition of Vipassana work at the body level. It is assumed that the mind exists in each and every living cell of our body and therefore to change the mind one has to work at one's body level. The brain is considered an important organ regulating consciousness, but there are many important functions of the mind that happen outside our heads, in a complex network of energy spread all over the body. Many complex tasks are precognitive and pre-linguistic and they tend to bypass our conscious awareness. They are mediated through internal body sensations and symbolic representations connecting our sensations with our thoughts.

Sensations as the roots of experience

We can understand our mind in terms of four domains – thoughts, emotions, sensations and behaviour, and this helps us understand four different types of introspection. These are reflecting our consciousness on to our thoughts, emotions, sensations and behaviour. Different schools of psychology emphasise different domains of our psyche. Cognitive therapists and psychoanalysts pay more attention to our thoughts and insights; experiential therapists feel that emotions are more important; and behaviourists would argue that behaviour should be studied as a subject matter in its own right if a change has to occur. Vipassana and other forms of mindfulness meditation encourage us to focus on inner body sensations.

We know that there are many experiences for which the corresponding thought forms do not exist, but it is inconceivable to think of an experience that does not involve inner body sensations. These sensations result from the contact of our five senses with the outside world, but they can also be triggered by the residual or resultant consciousness of past experiences, which remain dormant in the unconscious.

Reflecting our consciousness on to thought alone will take us to a certain point, but reflecting it on to the sensations will enable us to experience things in totality.

Such inner sensations are not experienced in the normal waking state, although they may be elicited when listening to music or in extreme conditions, such as fever, illness or fatigue. But these sensations are available at all times, being linked with the functioning of our unconscious mind, in each and every cell of the body. It is we who ordinarily fail to perceive them. Our failure to perceive them is similar to our inability to perceive stars in the sky in daytime although they are there all the time. We need a telescope to see them in daytime. The practice of Vipassana provides us with the mental telescope to feel these inner bodily sensations that are laid down as representations of our past actions or conditionings.

Each action, whether by word or thought or deed, leaves behind an active force called sankhara (also known as karma), which accumulates to the credit or debit "account" of the individual, depending upon the nature of the deed. The understanding of the three characteristics of impermanence, suffering and non-identification enables us to rid ourselves of the sankhara, which has accumulated in this account.

CHAPTER 11

Excerpts from Audio Sessions

Session 1: Causes of Stress

The first and foremost cause is the judgement that we make, judgements about different situations – in terms of good/bad, right/wrong, beautiful/ugly, intelligent/stupid, nice/nasty – about ourselves and about others. There is nothing wrong about making those judgements if those judgements are based on a realistic appraisal of the situation, they are not disproportionate and don't last any longer than needed.

I ask clients to visualise their lives not in terms of something solid but in terms of something fluid that is constantly shifting, constantly moving; things are disappearing, things are constantly changing outside of ourselves and within ourselves as well.

"Thinking about death in a positive way can help us accept it and be desensitised to it, which can be a remedy for a lot of clinical anxiety and depression.

Life appears much more beautiful in contrast when we have thought about death; things give more pleasure when we think of their existence coming to an end eventually.

The suffering of a normal person who doesn't suffer from psychological problems is also enormous. Those of us who can't come to terms with it are more likely to develop psychiatric problems.

Just because a thought is there in your mind it does not mean that it represents your true self. When you Google a word on the internet you find a drop down menu that tells you everything that has an association with that key word. In the same way, when a thought arises in the mind automatically, dozens of situations, thoughts, places and people are activated in the mind and they may not be related to who you are.

Letting go of a desire to control each and every bit of our lives can be a very liberating experience, and being open to what comes our way intended or unintended can be helpful.

Every relationship no matter how close it is has its own boundaries and beyond those boundaries we are all alone. We all are following our own life trajectory, which is different from that of other people; and from that perspective, being selfish would be quite normal as long as no exploitation is involved.

The next cause of stress is how we evaluate our lives, whether we see ourselves as a success or failure; and the answer to that question is both. We are successful and we are failures. We should refrain from making such global judgements, but go deeper and try to analyse in what ways we have been successful and failures.

Session 2: Understanding the Mind

We don't have to learn stress management the way we learn a foreign language. A foreign language has to be learnt from scratch, whereas management of stress is given to us naturally. It's very much like healing a physical injury. Like our body, the mind also knows how to heal itself.

It is the healthy part of the mind that deals with the stressful part of the mind. So we need at least a part of the mind that is free from emotions to deal with the emotional or stressful part of the mind, but that part of the mind should be emotionally neutral or stress free otherwise this work can't be done. I equate the healthy part of the mind with clean water that is needed to clean the dirty clothes. Coloured water or dirty water can't be used to wash clothes.

Distracting ourselves on to something else that doesn't remind us of the stress is generally unhelpful, except for certain situations where the stress is intolerable and continued exposure to it can cause further damage to our psyche. But apart from those situations, one has to stay connected with the inner stress in order for it to get worked on.

Our minds have an accelerator and a brake, very much like our cars; the sympathetic nervous system is the accelerator and the parasympathetic the brake. All physiological therapies, including yoga, biofeedback therapies, breathing exercises, etc., restore a balance between these two parts of the nervous system.

Session 3: Fine-Tuning Our Judgements and Dealing with Our Ghost Emotions

In mathematics, if 2 plus 2 is 4 then it can't be 6 or 8, but in psychology the two opposites can be equally true. For example, one can say we live in a caring and friendly world and the opposite of it, that the world is indifferent and uncaring, would be equally true. People are loving and caring and people are selfish; both these statements are equally true. There is an ultimate meaning in life and there is no ultimate meaning as everything disintegrates eventually; both these points of view would be equally true. I'm a successful person and I'm a failure; both are equally true depending upon the yardstick we use. This world is a beautiful place to live in and the saying that the beauty lies in the eyes of the beholder are equally true.

Whenever you get upset, ask yourself what judgements have I made here about myself and about others. You might find that six or seven times out of ten you have made a judgement and that judgement needs to be challenged before you accept it. The remaining three or four times it may be that you are experiencing a ghost emotion from your past. These ghost emotions are nothing but real emotions that you experienced in real life situations in the past, but are irrelevant now, although they still cause enormous suffering.

Whilst watching a sad film you might find yourself getting emotional, but when you say to yourself "Why am I getting emotional, it's just a film?" you can pull yourself out of the emotion. In a similar fashion, disidentification with our own negative thoughts and emotions can help us deal with our emotions better.

Session 4: Physiology of Stress

We can't control our heart rhythms directly, but there is a connection between our heart and our lungs, and by changing our breathing patterns we can change our heart rhythms.

Heart rate and stress levels go up when we breathe in and they go down when we breathe out. Therefore, breathing out for a longer period can reduce our stress levels.

Opera singers and yoga students are taught how to breathe abdominally and this practice promotes their health, both physical and mental.

One can alter one's brain wave pattern by way of listening to binaural beats. This is based on the principle of entrainment. In biofeedback therapy the brain is exposed to these binaural beats, which consist of a desired frequency wavelengths of sounds/lights. As a result the brain waves fall in sync with these waves leading to therapeutic benefits.

If you look carefully, you find that whenever we get stressed, mostly we are either thinking about something that happened in the past (i.e. a few minutes, hours, days or months ago) or something that is going to happen in the next few hours, days or months. If we live mostly in the present we can cut through a lot of stress.

Attention regulation is a very powerful tool in regulating one's emotions and stress.

Session 5: Philosophy and Psychoanalysis

We are always trying to escape from the inner reality due to its apparent scary nature and thereby cut ourselves off from the inner joys as well.

We tend to draw strength more from the hope of a better life than from what we have already got. This hope can be very useful in coping with one's everyday stress, but it shouldn't stop us from living in the present.

Because of our romanticised notions of human life we can't accept the reality of our existence and that of the external world, and this results in distortions of our perception of the reality. This distortion is the starting point of many psychological problems.

If distortion of the reality is the main problem, then authenticity is the antidote to it. Authenticity is acting in a manner that is in keeping with the inner reality; there are no false fronts.

Therapy is not all about feeling good; sometimes therapy makes people aware of the deeper human pain that they are unmindful of. Absorbing this pain into one's psyche can make the individual better able to deal with stress.

When we enter into an intimate relationship with others, there is a risk of losing one's authenticity. It's the risk that our actions will not be in keeping with our own inner reality, but rather with that of the realities of the other person, as we are taking their points of view into consideration and accommodating their existence into our psyche. A wise approach would be not to allow the other person to rob us of our inner space, and vice versa, and also to accept the other person without wanting to change them according to our needs and wishes.

All desires arise from an inner feeling of *lack*. This lack is not about lacking this or that, but about lack of connection with the deeper reaches of our psyche; call it soul, spirit, consciousness, universal mind, atman, the infinite, etc. No amount of external achievement will take away this feeling of lack.

Stoic branch of philosophy teaches us a way to develop fortitude so that we can overcome destructive emotions.

A stoic of virtue would amend his will to suit the world and remain – in the words of Epictetus (2004) – "sick and yet happy, in peril and yet happy, dying and yet happy, in exile and yet happy, in disgrace and yet happy".

Let us be cheerful and brave in the face of everything, reflecting that it is nothing of our own that perishes; we are the soul (inner consciousness) and not the body and the mind. Nothing grows on the soul that can give you agony when it is torn away.

Session 6: Well-Being Tools and Inner Peace

The tools discussed in the programme:

1. The experience of impermanence
2. Fine tuning one's judgements
3. Disidentification with one's ghost emotions
4. Writing an emotion diary
5. Attention regulation

6. Breath regulation
7. Biofeedback devices
8. Existential way of thinking
9. Learning to create positive issues out of nothing
10. How to be with other beings
11. Altruism
12. Being equanimous, detached from one's mind, but at the same time being loving and caring

If I were to tell you today that your life will be frozen from now on for eternity – which means that not an iota will change from how things are right now – would life be acceptable to you?

If you do not have a partner, you will not have a partner for eternity. If you do not have enough money, you will not have enough money for eternity. If you suffer from an illness, that illness will stay with you for eternity. If you have difficult relationships, those difficulties will continue for eternity. If your children are still small, they will remain small for eternity. Your age will remain frozen for eternity; if you are a young adult or an old man you will remain so for eternity. Will life be acceptable to you?

If your answer is yes, then perhaps you have learnt how to accept things and know how to access happiness and peace from within.

But if your answer to this question is no, this would mean that your acceptance of human life is not perfect – fair enough, there is nothing wrong with this; it is quite normal.

But I want you to visualise a scenario wherein I come back to you in a couple of years' time and ask you the same question. Is life acceptable to you? And I hope you would have done certain things to your psyche in those two years so that your acceptance of life has moved on.

CHAPTER 12

Tweets on Stress Management

From
@Kishore_Chandi

- My new year resolution – to understand my mind better i.e. solving all my problems by tackling their root causes.
- The mind has two parts to it – thinking, judging, feeling and reacting one; and the inner consciousness that doesn't judge or react but simply observes and reflects like a mirror.
- The art of being happy can't be perfected without knowing how to undo one's unhappiness.
- A good relationship should not be seen as a means to something, but an end in itself.
- Our relationships with fellow beings are much deeper than any problems we see in them.
- Mother Nature gives us relatives not according to our wants but according to our needs.
- No matter how old you are, you never stop needing your parents; it's about the need for genuine selfless love.

- If it is difficult for you to deal with someone, it must be difficult for them as well to deal with you, no matter how easy going you are.
- If people are against you it's not because of you, but because you are coming in the way of their life goals, please don't take it personally.
- Those who fail to compliment you on your little good acts must also be ignoring your little follies, don't these cancel each other out?
- Those who criticise you over little things must also be praising you for little things, don't these balance each other?
- The reasons that make you angry with someone are very much the same reasons someone else might feel compassionate towards them.
- Certain things may not matter to you, but if they matter to those who matter to you, you need to think if they should matter to you as well.
- Some of our relationships may not appear to have an ultimate meaning, but they stop us from falling into the abyss of meaninglessness.
- When you apparently don't need the other person and that person doesn't need you – the relationship can move into new positive dimensions.
- What a strange thing that we reach out to people who are indifferent to us and are indifferent to those who reach out to us.
- We can't predict the future accurately, so why be rigid about our judgments.
- Almost all our emotions result from our judgments made now or in the past.
- Our mind has the capacity to be judging and non-judging at the same time, we need both.
- Keeping the radio and television on in the background when not attending to it can mean you are not comfortable with your normal consciousness.
- You can change others only if you are able to change yourself in relation to them.
- Boredom means you are making a choice of neither connecting with the outer world nor with your inner one.
- When I can't face my inner world I seek distractions in the outer one, and when I can't cope with the outer world I hide in my inner one.
- You need an unhurried mind even for dealing with hurrying situations.
- I don't like people who don't like me; is this a fair emotion?

- I like certain people because they like me; is this a logical thought?
- Don't give people more knowledge, but your silence, presence and understanding.
- Doing the right thing is not enough, its timing is equally important.
- Those who are angry with us need more attention, not less.
- A slight good news and I am over the moon, and a little upset and I am down in the dumps; is this a good way to be?
- In therapy sometimes disowning our emotions is therapeutic, although normally it is a good idea to own them and take full responsibility.
- We can't wipe the slate of our mind clean, therefore non-identification with some of our thoughts and emotions would be the way forward.
- The painful emotions that you are experiencing in your mind now may not be a part of your real self but the mental garbage finding its way out.
- Be careful ! When stories of your undesirable behaviour are passed on they may be exaggerated.
- Whatever can be achieved through anger can also be achieved without using it, perhaps more effectively.
- Normally we deal with negative emotions when confronted with them. Meditation encourages us to seek them out and neutralise them in their hideouts.
- Negative emotions can't be undone by positive ones; they have to be dealt with on their own terms with the help of a neutral consciousness.
- We need to be free from our involvement with the positive emotions in order to work with the negative ones.
- Positive emotions don't automatically undo the negative ones, but they do give us the courage to face them and neutralise them.
- Trying to relax using your intellect is like trying to smooth disturbed water surfaces using your hand.
- The mind heals itself only when a part of it is emotionally neutral.
- Just observe your emotional reactions and let them subside before you act.
- We must learn to be okay at the times when nothing much is happening in our lives.
- We need both these skills – to be with the here and now; and to cut ourselves off from the present when we want.

- Our self-esteem is highly dependent upon how people treat us, it shouldn't be that way.
- The real self-esteem we should be looking for is the one that can survive indifference of others.
- We can be indifferent to the opinions of others only when we have found something inside us that is more gratifying than what they can offer.
- Stop trying to please people, just do the right thing and they will be pleased.
- It is important to know whether you are creating new depression every day or trying to deal with the existing one.
- Achieving a good work-life balance is not about adjusting the hours, but knowing what to do with the hours saved from work.
- Don't expect to feel the same as you did in the past, that's gone for ever. Look forward to being a different person in future.
- This moment is not very much different from all the magical moments from history and our good old days, and our dreams fulfilled.
- The thought that future is going to be better than the present can stop us from living fully in the present.
- To some, meditation may not give as much pleasure as the pleasures of the senses; but it does reduce the suffering related to them for sure.
- There is no need to worry about worldly losses or one's imperfections; our deeper consciousness has enough reserve to compensate for them.
- Less is more; talking less, wanting less, needing less, possessing less, reacting less, etc.
- A crisis in the external world may be the starting point for a spiritual journey.
- No matter how horrible a thought is, don't question its presence in your mind; just question your emotional reaction to it.
- The best definition of wisdom that I have come across is - the ability to foresee the consequences of one's actions.
- Acceptance has two components to it: letting go of the emotion and of the action. The first one is desirable, not the second one.
- The mind has two parts: observing self and experiencing self. Being an observer enables us to walk out of the experience of emotion.

- I can see that about 80% of my body symptoms are linked to my unconscious emotions; these links become apparent during meditation.
- Psychiatry as it exists today doesn't address the root cause of suffering.
- There is truth outside the boundaries of science, we should not ignore that; but at the same time not lose our foothold on the science.
- Alcohol and illicit drugs create a wall between us and our stress; they don't make the stress go away.
- Taking consciousness altering substances is like tempering with the engine of the car you are driving.
- Some overweight individuals seek comfort in food as it didn't come from a parent who was absent.
- Majority of psychiatric problems result from our inability to see the reality as it is, and involve its distorted perception.
- We distort the reality because it is not acceptable to us; and it is not acceptable because we have unrealistic definitions of what is normal.
- Enthusiasm is not something you have to create, it's given to you. Don't obstruct it with your judgments and negative emotions.
- Don't feel obliged to do whatever you have thought or planned, but do the job that you have put your hands on perfectly.
- Loneliness can be seen as an emotion that comes and goes away rather than a state one settles into due to lack of connection.
- Spiritual experiences can make our feelings of loneliness go away and our aloneness enjoyable.
- Our fear of death dissolves when we lose ourselves in the infinite and the eternal.
- Acquiring the real knowledge is not like filling an empty pot, but dissolving oneself into it, like the ice melting into the sea water.
- Seeking solitude / "me time" is not being selfish but responding to our basic psychological need.
- Every thought and every emotion has a corresponding molecule inside our body: working both at the body and mind levels can be more effective in stress management.
- Underneath our desires and attempts to fulfil them there is also a desire to overcome them.
- Psychological growth is possible only when we are willing to disagree with our own thoughts.

- The biggest of all skills in de-stressing oneself is the ability to distance oneself from one's own thoughts.
- Accessing inner peace is like digging for gold; it requires working with the gravel, mud and rocks in the mind.
- Words, both spoken and heard, can pollute our inner consciousness which rejoices in silence.
- Every mental activity should arise from and end in silence.
- When things don't go right it's time to build character, wisdom, strength and equanimity.
- Reading more can enrich your mind, but the inner consciousness doesn't need any enrichment from outside.
- The person who can't surrender to nature when needed is like a traveller who is carrying the luggage on his shoulders even after boarding a train.
- God's chosen ones may not necessarily be the ones who are in the limelight; some who live or choose to live in obscurity may be equally or more blessed.
- Make your inner self your guide, teacher, therapist, philosopher and your God.

REFERENCES

- Anliker, J (1977) Biofeedback from the perspective of cybernetics and systems science. IN Beatty J, Legewie, H editors. Biofeedback and Behaviour, New York Plenum Press.
- Assagioli, R (1986) Psychosynthesis: A Manual of Principles and Techniques, Turnstone Press Ltd, UK.
- Brihadaranyaka Upanishad (1983) Swami Krishnanada, Divine Life Society, India
- Buber, M (1923) I and Thou, English translation 1937, Charles Scribner's Sons, reprint continuum International Publishing Group, 2004.
- Cannon, WB (1929) Organisation of Physiological Homeostasis, Physiological Review, 9(3) 399-431.
- Chandiramani, K (2014) www.undoyourstress.com
- Davidson, RJ (1995) Cerebral Asymmetry, MIT Press, Cambridge, MA.
- Deurzen, E van (1997) Everyday Mysteries, Routledge, London.
- Epictetus (2004) Enchiridion, The Dover Publications Inc.
- Freud, S (1915) The Unconscious (Das Unbewusste) translated by Graham Frankland, 2005 Penguin Classics.
- Gardner, H (1983) Frames of Mind: The Theory of Multiple Intelligences, Basic Books.

- Gevirtz, RN, Lehrer, P (2003) Resonant Frequency Heart Rate Biofeedback, In Schwartz, M, Andrasik, F editors, Biofeedback: A Practitioners Guide, Guilford Press, London.
- Ghalib (2003) Ed Russell Ralph, The Oxford India Ghalib: Life, Letters and Ghazals, Oxford University Press, New Delhi.
- Grillon, C (2005) Anxiety Disorder: Psychological Aspects. In Sadock BJ and Sadock VA, editors, Comprehensive Textbook of Psychiatiry, eighth edition, Lippincott Williams and Williams; Philadelphia.
- Heidegggger, M (1927) Being and Time, trans J Macquarrie and E S Robinson, London, Harper and Row 1962.
- Jung CG (1959) in the Basic Writings of C G Jung, Random House, reprinted 1990, Princeton University Press.
- Katie, B (2002) Loving what is: Four Questions That Can Change Your Life, Ebury Press.
- Kierkegaard, S (1849) The Sickness Unto Death, trans. H Hong and E Hong, Princeton NJ: Princeton University Press 1980.
- Kornfield, J (2000) After the Ecstasy, the Laundry: How the Heart Grows Wise on the Spiritual Path, Radom House, London.
- Lacan, J (1977) Ecrits: A selection, London, Tavistock.
- Montaigne, M (1991) The Essays of Michael de Montaigne, translated and edited by MA Screech, London: Allen Lane.
- Nietzsche, F (1883) Thus Spoke Zarathustra, trans. R J Hollingdale, Harmondsworth, Penguin, 1961.
- Orchs, L (1992) EEG Treatment of Addictions, Biofeedback, 20 (1), 8-16.
- Peniston EC and Kulkosky, PJ (1990) Alcoholic Personality and alpha-theta brain wave training. Medical Psychotherapy, 3; 37-55.
- Prochaska, JO. DiClemente, CC & Norcross, JC (1992) In Search of How People Change. Applications to Addictive Behaviour, Am Psychologist 47, 1102.
- Rinpoche, S (1992) The Tibetan book of living and dying, Harper San Francisco.
- Sartre, JP (1944) No Exit and Three other Plays, Vintage.
- Skinner, BF & Vaughan ME (1983) Enjoy Old Age, W. W. Norton & Company, London

- Shakesheare, W (1992) Hamlet, ed. Cedric Watts, Wordsworth Classics.
- Schwartz, MS, Olson RP (2003) Historical Perspective on the field of biofeedback and applied psychophysiology, In Schwartz M and Andrasik F, editors, Biofeedback: A Practitioners Guide, London, Guilford Press.
- Selye, H (1956) The Stress of Life, McGraw-Hill, New York.
- Storr, A (1997) Solitude, Harper Collins.
- Tillich, P (1952) The Courage to Be, New Haven CT: Yale University Press.
- The Bhagavad Gita (1994) A new translation by W J Johnson, Oxford University Press, New York.
- The Dhammapada (1987) translated by Carter, JR and Mahindra, P, Oxford University Press, New York.
- Yalom, ID (2002) The Gift of Therapy, Harper Collins Publishers, New York.
- Todres, L (2002) Globalisation and the complexity of self: the relevance of Psychotherapy. Existential Analysis: Journal of the Society for Existential Analysis, 13, 98-105.

Printed in Great Britain
by Amazon